# MOUNTAIN
# BIKE

G000255270

# Northumberland

## by Derek Purdy

ERNEST

The Ernest Press
www.ernest-press.co.uk

Published by the Ernest Press 2005
© Copyright Derek Purdy

1st edition published in 1992 & reprinted in 1996

British Library Cataloguing-in-Publication Data has been registered
with the British Library at Wetherby and is available on request

ISBN 0948153 78 4

Typeset by Phil Hodgkiss Design and Print

Produced by Elkar-mccgraphics, Bilbao

**Disclaimer:**

### *Revision of grading system.*

Having used Tim King's system of grading during the revision of the Inverness guide last year, I felt that a more subjective system for 'Northumberland' might be a good idea. Inspired by Tim's thinking, each route is allotted points according to the predominant type of surface, ascent, topographical conditions, length and perhaps a bonus point or two – just to add the personal touch! The scoring goes roughly as follows:

| | | |
|---|---|---|
| *SURFACE:* | Metalled road | 1 |
| | Forest/farm/estate road/rail trail | 2 |
| | Four-wheel-drive/moorland track | 3 |
| | Firm path | 4 |
| | Mud/grass/moorland/dune paths | 5 |
| | | |
| *ASCENT:* | Flat | 1 |
| | Gentle short climbs | 2 |
| | Gentle longer climbs | 3 |
| | Medium short climbs | 4 |
| | Medium longer climbs | 5 |
| | Energetic (gut busting) short climbs | 6 |
| | Energetic (appalling) longer climbs | 7 |
| | | |
| *GENERAL CONDITIONS:* | | |
| | Low level sheltered | 1 |
| | Low level exposed | 2 |
| | Mid level sheltered | 3 |
| | Mid level exposed | 4 |
| | High level | 5 |
| | | |
| *LENGTH:* | Up to 10 km | 1 |
| | 11 – 20 km | 2 |
| | 21 – 30 km | 3 |
| | 31 – 40 km | 4 |
| | Over 40 km | 5 |

## ROUTES IN NUMERICAL ORDER

## NORTHUMBERLAND by 'REGIONS'

*NORTHEAST – as far south as the River Coquet (excl. the Cheviot Hills)*

*CHEVIOT HILLS*

## RIDES IN ORDER OF DIFFICULTY

| grade | length (km) | no. | name |
|---|---|---|---|
| 8 | 19.68 | 34 | Lindisfarne or Holy Island |
| 9 | 17.72 | 18 | Boulmer |
| 10 | 12.85 | 1 | The Hagg |
| 10 | 18.02 | 40 | Featherstone, South Tyne |
| 11 | 27.55 | 33 | Butterwell Bridleways |
| 12 | 31.1 | 23 | Wansbeck Wanderings |
| 13 | 14.00 | 22 | Harwood Forest |

| | | | |
|---|---|---|---|
| 13 | 25.27 | 7 | Ford Moss & Doddington |
| 14 | 11.42 | 20 | Rothbury Carriage Drive |
| 14 | 23.59 | 39 | Makemerich & Frolic |
| 14 | 34.95 | 27 | Bloody Bush Toll Road |
| 15 | 7.89 | 3 | Alwinton Short Cut |
| 15 | 10.32 | 19 | Stobb Cross Loop |
| 15 | 12.61 | 6 | Circuit of Greensheen Hill |
| 15 | 15.32 | 21 | Blanchland Moor |
| 15 | 16.84 | 5 | Wooler Water & Coldmartin Loughs |
| 15 | 18.11 | 2 | Powburn County Roads |
| 16 | 16.50 | 4 | Milfield and Coldside Hill |
| 16 | 16.87 | 24 | Stobb Cross Extension |
| 16 | 44.24 | 29 | Alnwick – Coast & Country |
| 17 | 19.00 | 12 | Ingram & Alnham |
| 17 | 20.89 | 25 | Moors of Greenrigg & Eshells |
| 18 | 7.53 | 9 | Barrowburn Loop |
| 18 | 22.29 | 36 | Percy's Moss |
| 18 | 43.09 | 31 | Cross Border Route |
| 19 | 25.56 | 26 | Vallum |
| 19 | 27.06 | 37 | Roads Round Rubbingstob Hill |
| 19 | 32.77 | 30 | Hexhamshire Common |
| 19 | 58.24 | 32 | Kielder Forest Drive & The Wheel Causeway |
| 20 | 15.70 | 11 | Bewick Moor |
| 20 | 17.26 | 8 | Wooler Common & Broadstruther |
| 20 | 19.26 | 10 | Langlee Crags & Threestoneburn |
| 20 | 21.67 | 15 | Middle Route |
| 20 | 25.4 | 14 | Ingram, Bleakhope & Alnham |
| 20 | 36.94 | 35 | Watergate |
| 21 | 22.21 | 13 | Deel's Hill |
| 21 | 29.62 | 16 | The Street |
| 21 | 36.70 | 28 | Long Cross |
| 21 | 37.70 | 17 | Clennell Street & Salters Road |
| 21 | 39.64 | 38 | Castles, Climbs & Clarts |

| Total score | Route grade | Ride numbers |
|---|---|---|
| Up to 12 | Sporting | 1, 18, 23, 33, 34, 40 |
| 13 – 16 | Energetic | 2, 3, 4, 5, 6, 7, 19, 20,21, 22, 24, 27, 29,39 |
| 17 – 20 | Strenuous | 8, 9, 10, 11, 12, 14, 15, 25, 26, 30, 31, 32, 35, 36, 37 |
| 21 and over | Expert | 13, 16, 17, 28, 38 |

*Originally there was an 'Easy' grade, but none of the routes qualified!*

## ACKNOWLEDGEMENTS

This updated and augmented colour version of the guide should really have an enormous list of acknowledgements – as one would expect to accumulate over the thirteen years since the appearance of the original edition – but hopefully it will suffice to thank all who have contributed in so many different ways. You know who you are, possibly some would not even want to admit it! Of the original 'epics' team, Malcolm Williams, whose idea it was to write it all down, Steve Bell, noted for the latest in bike technology, and Pam (who has decided after all these years she doesn't like off-road riding) still turn out with the author and can be found lurking in the depths of Upper Coquetdale.

I am most grateful to the Northumberland Estates for permission to use their private road from Hartside to Alnhammoor at the head of the Ingram Valley, and delighted to convey the wishes of the Estate that they hope that mountain bikers will enjoy this stretch. This is a permissive route, so please stick to the road and the little path at Alnhammoor. Thank you.

# Route Outlines

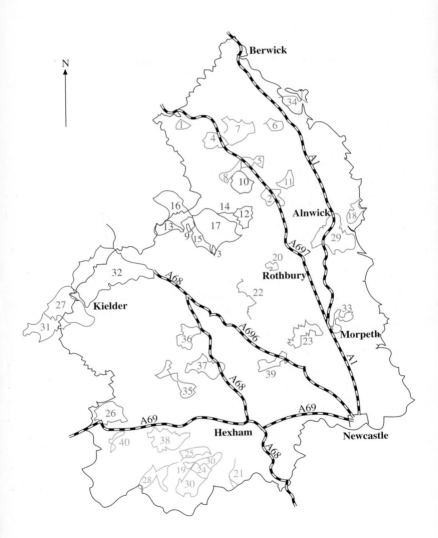

## INTRODUCTION

The object of this book is to give a little guidance to new mountain bikers, or to extend the range of others. Having tried a few of the routes described, there is no doubt that riders will start to devise their own loops, or through routes, of a length and type to suit their own style and ability; but you are earnestly implored to try most of these at some time if only to become familiar with the differences between what is marked on an Ordnance Survey map and what is actually on the ground.

Northumberland is England's farthest north, and one of the best-kept tourist and mountain biking secrets in the country. Although only moderate in height, the Cheviot Hills have a rounded and confusing character – enjoy but respect them. Please remember that no matter how wild or remote any area of Northumberland may appear, it is someone's working environment. Forestry, hill-farming or moor management in connection with shooting interests encompass all of the areas most attractive to us. Respect this and foster good relations between mountain bikers and the rural community.

Unlike walkers' guides, which can be read as you travel, pausing literally at any step along the way, **I recommend that you read the route in this book in advance and transfer it to the relevant Ordnance Survey map using the Plotting Plan.**

### Public Rights of Way

Cyclists have a right of way over bridleways provided they give way to walkers and horses, and of course on tracks of higher status. e.g. old county roads. An increasing number of old county roads that have not been given a tarmac surface are appearing on Ordnance Survey maps. The Hagg route is testament to this. If in doubt visit the County Rights of Way Department and examine their definitive maps.

All of the routes in this book have been prepared in consultation with the definitive maps. While I have taken the greatest care to ensure the legality of all the routes in this guide, things do change. And it is emphasised that you use any route entirely at your own risk.

## Maps

Despite their shortcomings, Ordnance Survey maps are the best available. Unfortunately, from an expanse point of view, Northumberland is a huge county. Seven Landranger maps are required to cover all these routes, while you will need 8 of the Explorer series. This is one of the reasons for the sketch-maps accompanying each route. While I claim no great cartographical skill, they do cover the entire route. Used with the appropriate Landranger, which should always be carried in case you need to escape from the route for whatever reason, the sketch-maps will get you around. Where necessary some features on the sketch-maps have been greatly exaggerated.

## Equipment & Safety

*FIRST-AID.* Buy and carry a copy of 'First-aid on mountains' by Steve Bollen MB, FRCS, published by the British Mountaineering Council, at 95p. If you become involved in an accident situation, try to keep calm. A mountain biker will be able to get off the hill to seek help far quicker than any pedestrian – but do not get carried away. Becoming a casualty of over-enthusiasm, particularly on the downhills, will not help. A comprehensive first-aid kit is a good idea if you are involved in a party of any size, but may seem a bit over the top as a personal item. Be sensible, carry something that can relieve immediate problems. I suggest a small roll of sticking plaster (that can also be used to repair bags, clothes, glasses!) and a small tube of antiseptic cream as an absolute minimum. It is amazing what a dab of cream can fix.

*PERSONAL IDENTIFICATION.* Always carry something about you to aid the rescue services just in case the worst happens, particularly if you travel alone.

*SAFETY ON THE HILLS.* On the more remote routes you should act as a mountaineer first, and a cyclist second. Again the British Mountaineering Council has an excellent little booklet 'Safety on mountains'. Simply modify some of the advice to mountain biking, and adopt the rest. As a mountain biker, you should be self-sufficient on the hills for both yourself and your bike. Sharing equipment can ease the load but make sure you have got what YOU need. It is useless blaming deficiencies on others when you are out there. Last items are a whistle, compass, and a Poly Bag or Survival Blanket – just in case.

## The Bike

Do not buy a bike that is too big. Male or female, you need three inches crotch clearance at the crossbar when standing over the bike. Many times out on the fell you will need to put a foot down and there will be nothing there – do not get caught out. As an example, my inside leg measurement is 32, my road bike frame size is 23, but my mountain bike is only 18.5.

*MAINTENANCE.* Bike parts can be broken, get caught on a rock, or simply wear out at any time, but try to minimise the risk of this by first-class maintenance. Do not try to make anything 'last' one more trip, or postpone any jobs that need done. You can guarantee it will let you down when you are farthest from home. Any time spent cleaning, greasing or lubricating is time well spent, and it is amazing what you will spot when doing this. Brakes and tyres need special attention. Make sure you can stop. Check your tyres for flints and thorns as well as pressure before you set off. If you have not had them off the rims for a while, take them off, give them a good dose of talcum powder, and give the tubes every chance to do their work. While you have the tyres off, check the rims for bashes and little slivers of metal sliced off by stone damage.

*TOOLS.* Your toolkit will reflect your level of preparation. My toolkit comprises:
Pump – better than a compressed air cartridge because it will inflate an infinite number of tubes, but slower. A cartridge will shave minutes off a

tube change, which could be quite important in an exposed situation in cold weather. I take one of each! Spare tube for speed of change. Small adjustable wrench, also doubles as a spoke key. Suitable selection of Allen keys. One tyre lever – something else will double as the other one. Chain splitter. Puncture repair kit, just in case you get 2 or more punctures. Piece of soft wire, 1001 uses. Spare toe strap – also use it as an auxiliary tie for undersaddle tool bag. Pair of minipliers – they really help if your hands are frozen. Cloth – wrap the whole lot in your wiping rag.

*LIGHTS & REFLECTORS.* If you ride anywhere on a public highway after lighting up time you need lights and reflectors. Riding off-road over tough terrain in the dark is hazardous to say the least, but can add a new dimension to your routes! Invest in a good set of road lights. A Petzl head torch is a good stand by.

CYCLE COMPUTER. A cycle computer is a great navigational aid, especially on featureless moorland or in dense forestry with limited view. Choose 'Km' option for your display and you are tied directly to Ordinance Survey whose grid squares all have 1 kilometre sides regardless of which scale you use. Estimating distances between junctions or features on the map is relatively easy, half square is 0.5 km, three quarters is 0.75 km, diagonally across a square is 1.5 km. In time you will become quite an expert. You then simply zero the 'trip distance' on your computer, relate your estimate to the computer reading as you ride along and look for the junction or feature when you estimate comes up.

## Clothing
Your enjoyment of mountain biking will be greatly enhanced if you invest in proper padded cycling shorts from the outset. Synthetic chamois is my preference; it needs no maintenance other than regular washing, and dries quite quickly.

Above all, clothing must be comfortable. The northern climate is so variable, particularly up high that your riding wardrobe needs to be able to cope with everything from near tropical sunshine to quasi-Arctic conditions in any one day! The answer is layers. Garments you can add or discard according to your body heat. Firms such as Polaris has given very serious consideration to the needs of the mountain biker and have produced some ideal garments. These should be able to keep water out, keep heat in, and to allow water vapour to escape. Membrane fabrics such as Goretex go some way towards achieving this, but mountain biking is such a high energy sport that even these materials cannot cope with all the moisture we produce. 1 have found the answer in fleeces of various densities and weaves. They wick the moisture away from your skin, are reasonably waterproof and, as soon as it stops raining, will dry out as you ride in quite a short time. When the rain really tipples down you will obviously need a waterproof shell garment that is easy to stow and carry and will not lose its characteristics when folded for long periods. Polaris have produced a Pertex windshell which, while not claiming to be totally waterproof, boasts all of these characteristics: repulses rain with remarkable efficiency, and packs down to a parcel the size of your fist.

Up to now legs have been a problem! Although there is not the same degree of heat loss from the lower limbs, in winter they can become so cold that they cease to function properly. Buy a good set of salopettes/ biblongs, fleece or windproof fleece lined. Even a pair of quilted bottoms have a proven track record for the bike mid-winter. Now there is no excuse for staying in the house!

Last, but most important, wear a helmet. There is no choice. Wear one. The soft-shell polystyrene types are super lightweight and easy to get used to. Buy one that looks good, so you will wear it. Please wear one.

**Abbreviations:**

| | |
|---|---|
| R | RIGHT |
| L | LEFT |
| SO | STRAIGHT ON |
| TL | TURN LEFT |
| TR | TURN RIGHT |
| TJ | T-JUNCTION |
| XR | CROSSROADS |

## GLOSSARY

| | |
|---|---|
| **bait:** | refreshments, packed lunch |
| **bastle houses:** | fortified house common in the Borders |
| **canny (beasts):** | gentle, harmless |
| **clarts/clarty:** | sticky mud |
| **conies:** | rabbits |
| **galloways:** | small strong packhorses |
| **gliff**: | fright |
| **gulley:** | ditch, channel worn by running water |
| **linn:** | waterfall/steep-sided valley |
| **levee:** | raised embankment |
| **lonnen:** | unsurfaced lane |
| **lough:** | lake |
| **Moonters:** | Team Moont, Scottish mountain bike team |
| **pele:** | fortified Border tower |
| **plodge:** | wade |
| **Porcupine:** | Onza Porcupine mountain bike tyres |
| **set your neck:** | break your neck |
| **Snipes:** | Simonside Snipes, Northumbrian mountain bike team |
| **stell**: | circular sheepfold |
| **whinnies:** | whin bushes, gorse |
| **wicket:** | small gate |

## SKETCH-MAP SYMBOLS

Bridleway – well-defined

Bridleway – poorly defined

Track or Unsurfaced Road

Tarmac Road

Railway

Stream or River

Wall

Fence

Crags

Buildings ■ ■ + etc

Trees

Col or Pass – Height in metres    Hawsen Col ⟶ 376 ⟵

Summit – Height in metres    Barrow Law ▲ 419

Ford

Gate    G

Cattle Grid

Stile    ⟨

Post    P

***The Hagg.*** *Farm Cottages at West Learmouth. In many places this type of dwelling has been sold. Here every house has at least one person involved with agriculture.*

**18**

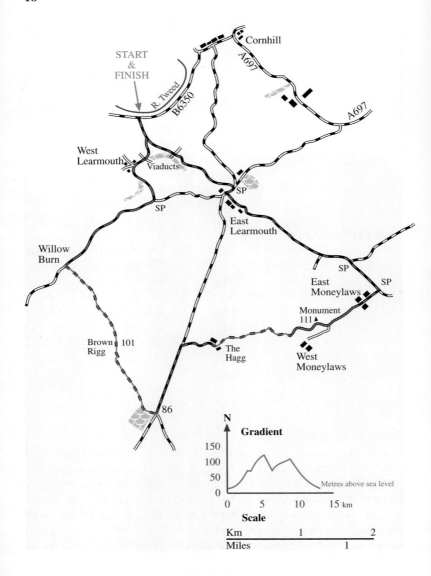

START & FINISH

R. Tweed

B6350

Cornhill

A697

A697

West Learmouth

Viaducts

SP

SP

East Learmouth

Willow Burn

SP

SP

East Moneylaws

Monument 111▲

Brown Rigg 101

The Hagg

West Moneylaws

86

**N**

**Gradient**

150
100
50
0

Metres above sea level

0          5          10          15 km

**Scale**

Km          1          2
Miles          1

# 1 The Hagg

| | |
|---|---|
| **Grade** | 10 Sporting |
| **12.85 km** | **(7.98 Miles)** |
| **2.98 km** | Tractor Track |
| **1.52 km** | Farm Road |
| **8.35 km** | Tarmac |
| **High Point:** | East Moneylaws 111 m |
| **Maps:** | Ordnance Survey, Landranger 74 Kelso & Coldstream, Explorer 339 Kelso, Coldstream |
| **Facilities:** | None on route, but ample in nearby Cornhill and Coldstream |

## PLOTTING PLAN

| *START:* | Approach | Map Reference | Depart |
|---|---|---|---|
| B6350 Learmouth Road End | – | 74/849$^{1}/_{2}$385 | SSE |
| East Learmouth | NE | 862374 | SE |
| East Moneylaws Road End | NW | 881362 | SW |
| Old County Road | ENE | 870$^{1}/_{2}$356 | W |
| The Hagg | NE | 861$^{1}/_{2}$354 | W |
| Spot Height 86m | NNE | 853$^{1}/_{2}$344$^{1}/_{2}$ | NW |
| Willow Burn | SE | 841$^{1}/_{2}$364 | NE |
| West Learmouth Viaduct | SW | 851379 | NE |
| *FINISH:* | | | |
| Learmouth Road End | SSE | 849$^{1}/_{2}$385 | – |

## Route Description

This is the easiest route in the book: designed to give the absolute beginner a taste of off-road riding, an introduction to map reading and an example of an old county road which is impossible to discern on the map as a Right of Way – and which even has a section omitted on the Landranger series! The bridleway over Brown Rigg is also one of the most entertaining in the county; the Learmouth railway viaducts are beautiful pieces of architecture and you are afforded great views of the Tweed

Valley from the heights above The Hagg. In fact it is well worth a ride round even if you are not a beginner.

### Learmouth Road End to The Hagg

There are a couple of compacted earth laybys near Learmouth road end. Please do not park in the fishermen's enclosure at the green hut. Depart SSE towards, then under, the eastern viaduct and onwards to the junction at the War Memorial where we TR. Turn first L up past East Learmouth farm and follow this road for just over 2 km until you reach East Moneylaws. Here we TR to follow the old county road through the farm and across to The Hagg. The old road bears R before West Moneylaws, assumes a stony surface and climbs to the highest point on the route, 111m. Just around the summit bend there is a small monument bearing the inscription, *"Erected AD 1878 in front of the house in which the Rev. Ralph Erskine was born AD 1685. He was the son of the Rev. Henry Erskine, Presbyterian minister of Cornhill from 1649 till the Bartholomew Ejectment in 1662. He was also one of the founders of the Scottish Secession Church and minister in Dunfermline from 1711 till his death in 1752. He attained great celebrity as a preacher and author."* Beyond the monument the road zooms down to a collection of gates where we TR along the stream, following the poles. At the next gate we TL and hug the hedge on a track that is a bit lumpy but carries us directly to The Hagg. Wiggle through the farm and make your way up to the TJ where we TL.

### The Hagg to The Tweed

Our bridleway starts off NW from the next XR and climbs gently over Brown Rigg. The going can be a bit sticky in wet conditions, but the big consolation is that the far end is 32m lower than the beginning so it is mostly downhill. Do not get too carried away because some of the ruts are quite deep. When you reach the tarmac at Willow Burn, TR. Follow the triangle where the SP points the way to West Learmouth, then down under the western viaduct and back to the banks of the Tweed.

***Powburn Country Roads.*** *Typical of the off-road sections, this stretch past Nova Scotia is eminently rideable at any time of year, as shown by Chris & Ted Hall.*

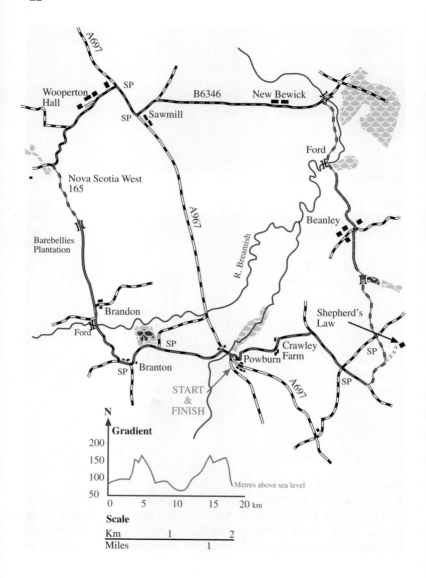

A697

SP

Wooperton
Hall

B6346

New Bewick

SP
Sawmill

Ford

Nova Scotia West
165

A967

Beanley

Barebellies
Plantation

R. Breamish

Brandon

Ford

Shepherd's
Law

SP

Branton

SP

Crawley
Farm

Powburn

SP

A697

SP

START
&
FINISH

**N**

**Gradient**

200
150
100
50

Metres above sea level

0        5        10        15        20 km

**Scale**

Km              1              2
Miles                    1

## 2 Powburn County Roads

| | |
|---|---|
| **Grade** | 15 Energetic |
| **18.11 km** | **(11.25 miles)** |
| **7.57 km** | Farm/Estate Roads |
| **10.54 km** | Tarmac |
| **High Points:** | Nova Scotia West 165m, Shepherds Law Road 168m |
| **Maps:** | Ordnance Survey, Landrangers 75 Berwick-upon-Tweed, 81 Alnwick & Morpeth, Explorer 332 Alnwick & Amble |
| **Facilities:** | Pub and Cafe in Powburn |

### PLOTTING PLAN

| *START:* | Approach | Map Reference | Depart |
|---|---|---|---|
| The Plough, Powburn | – | 81/062$^{1}/_{2}$163$^{1}/_{2}$ | NNW |
| Branton | E | 044$^{1}/_{2}$163 | NW |
| *Alternative START:* | | | |
| grass carpark, Brandon | S | 040170 | N |
| Nova Scotia West | S | 035190 | N |
| A697 | SW | 75/043$^{1}/_{2}$205 | SE |
| B6346 | SW | 049$^{1}/_{2}$203 | E |
| New Bewick Bridge | SW | 076203$^{1}/_{2}$ | SE |
| Breamish Ford | NNE | 81/077194 | SSE |
| Beanley | NNW | 081$^{1}/_{2}$183 | S |
| Shepherds Law Road | NNW | 085$^{1}/_{2}$163$^{1}/_{2}$ | SW |
| Crossroads | SE | 079162 | NW |
| Crawley Farm | N | 069$^{1}/_{2}$165$^{1}/_{2}$ | WSW |
| *FINISH:* | | | |
| The Plough, Powburn | NNW | 062$^{1}/_{2}$163$^{1}/_{2}$ | – |

### Route Description

When you are searching for new mountain bike routes the natural tendency is to gravitate towards bridleways. But there is some good riding on old county roads. These are thoroughfares that might have been surfaced, but you usually need a good 4x4 to negotiate them. As a starter route or a 'not too rough' option, they are great for mountain biking. These roads were not surfaced with tarmac because an easier alternative was often available, or fords which were liable to flood comprised part of the route. And this is precisely why the eastern and western legs of this loop were neglected. Nowadays, only the farmers and now mountain bikers, use them. What remains are quiet, and by our standards, well-surfaced tracks. To be honest, I thoroughly enjoyed this tour and formed the opinion that some of the finest views of the Cheviot Hills are afforded by the elevated parts of the route, particularly near the end – from Shepherds Law and Crawley Farm before you plummet down the final hill.

## Powburn to Wooperton

Parking is limited in Powburn, but the carpark of The Plough is ideally situated. In return for the facility it would be nice if you gave the pub some custom. There is more space at Brandon. Set off NNW from the pub, taking care on the short stretch of main road. Cross the bridge and TL immediately into a little lane between the speed derestriction signs. Head W to Branton and follow the main road through the hamlet then TR towards the ford. Both roads at the junction bear 'No Through Road Signs', neither of which is actually true. But as mentioned earlier the average family car would not make it. Brandon ford has a loose bottom – great entertainment in the summer, but not the thing to attempt early on a winter's day. The bridge is a sensible, rideable alternative, and also lets you see the route stretching ahead up the hill to the N. There are 80 metres of tarmac before the start of the well-compacted climb that tops out at 156m opposite the intriguingly named Barebellies Plantation. The mind boggles!

The road drops down to wiggle across a little stream then climbs up the side of the fields to the top of Nova Scotia West at 165m. We join tarmac – if you can see it through the mud – and TR at the 3 gates. Follow the poles down a narrow, twisting hill to a more significant road that takes us E to Wooperton Hall and the A697. The farm at Wooperton is complete.

It has all the classic features. A horse usually monitors progress from the stable on the left. There is an ancient manual petrol pump on the right, and if you look behind you will see the duckpond which boasted a couple of Canada geese the day I passed.

## Wooperton to Powburn

Turn R at the A697, first L onto the B6346 at Wooperton Sawmill which used to be the station. Wind up the big gears all the way to New Bewick Bridge. Immediately before the bridge TR again onto our second old county road. This one has a totally different feel. It follows the river closely then crosses the grass pastures to the new footbridge and ford to re-cross the River Breamish. This ford has a concrete bottom, is totally without character, and is sited 50 metres downstream from its predecessor. The old crossing, as shown on the map upstream of the bridge, was a serious test. I recall in my rallying days practising with a Mercedes Benz Gelendewagen, entering the water perhaps a little too sportily only to find the river over the bonnet and literally washing the windscreen. Every credit to the beast, it swam through and delighted me by clawing its way up the far side onto dry land. Heed the depth gauge! Follow the farm road up to Beanley. Jink R then L across the tarmac again, and continue S towards Shepherds Law. En route you should see wildfowl at the pond in the dip. Go past an ancient pre-cast concrete drinking trough at the last gate before crossing the road again. Climb up the bridleway to the Shepherds Law road. You might question this last climb on the old road beneath Shepherds Law when we could simply TR at the XR – but the extra elevation provided seems to enhance the terrific views of the Cheviots, and of course there is a fun little flash down the loose lane back to the tarmac. Turn NW through the XR then L to Crawley Farm, where one should pause momentarily for the last panorama before hurtling down to Powburn.

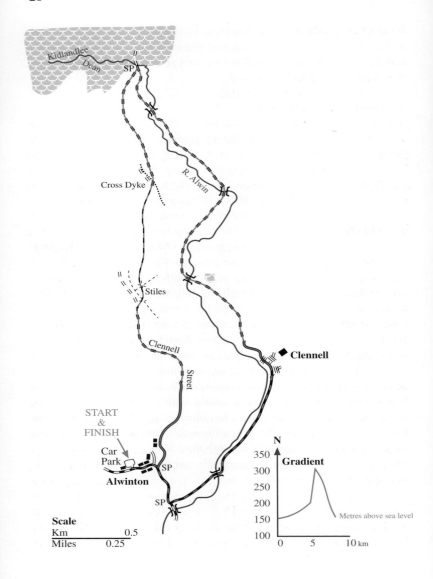

Kidlandlee
Dean
SP

Cross Dyke

R. Alwin

Stiles

Clennell

Clennell

Street

START
&
FINISH

Car
Park

SP

Alwinton

SP

**Scale**
Km _____ 0.5
Miles _____ 0.25

N

**Gradient**

350
300
250
200
150
100

Metres above sea level

0          5          10 km

# 3 Alwinton Short Cut

| | |
|---|---|
| **Grade** | 15 Energetic |
| **7.89 km** | **(4.9 Miles)** |
| **3.21 km** | Moorland Track/Path |
| **2.71 km** | Farm/Estate Road |
| **1.97 km** | Tarmac |
| **High Point:** | Diagonal Track Summit (Cross Dyke) 305m |
| **Maps:** | Ordnance Survey, Landranger 80 Cheviot Hills & Kielder Water, Explorer OL 16 Cheviot Hills |
| **Facilities:** | Pub, grub & camping – Rose & Thistle, Alwinton and Clennell Hall. Chalets & caravan site, Clennell Hall. |

## PLOTTING PLAN

| *START:* | Approach | Map Reference | Depart |
|---|---|---|---|
| Car Park, Alwinton | – | 80/920063 | E |
| Clennell | S | 927073 | NW |
| Kidlandlee Dean | SSE | 920091½ | SSW |
| Cross Dyke | N | 920½080 | S |
| Clennell Street | N | 920072 | SE |
| *FINISH:* | | | |
| Car Park, Alwinton | E | 920063 | – |

## Route Description

Many people are intimidated by the Cheviot Hills because of their wandering valleys and rounded summits, and rightly so. But once you get a feel for them the whole area opens up. I do not think familiarity would ever breed contempt in the Cheviots, because as your knowledge of them increases, so does your appreciation of their muted grandeur. In this respect I hope this 'starter' route in the heart of these northern hills will give you a flavour of them, and a firm base on which to build. The ride up the red road of the Alwin Valley puts you in real hill country in no time at all. Then the climb up the diagonal track from Kidlandlee Dean brings new rewards for every metre gained. Traversing the route at different times of day will bring different emphasis to the surrounding tops, and different times of year will bring different pleasures. But it can tease you too. One windy January day I stood at the summit of the diagonal track, at the Cross Dyke, waiting for the cloud on Cheviot and Hedgehope to blow over, until it became too cold to hold the camera still, and was forced to abandon the classic winter shot. On the other hand, I have sat on the hillside so long on a sunny day that all thoughts of serious mountain biking have evaporated.

### Alwinton to Kidlandlee Dean

Retrace from the carpark back through the village then TL into the road that leads to Clennell. Now follow this road all the way to Kidlandlee Dean. The first kilometre is good tarmac and a very pleasant run alongside the River Alwin. Then as you pass Clennell, the tarmac gives way to the red felsite, quarried at Harden, Biddlestone, just around the hill to the E. The red road now winds up the valley crossing three bridges before we turn for home. This is a good clean river with a huge catchment area and the wildlife reflects this. You will most likely see an old heron (they always look old to me) flapping away ahead of you, and there is a good chance of spotting a dipper. But pause on one of the bridges and consider the green of the weed in the water which even in winter is bright – surely the sign of stream in good order.

Just before entering the forest there is a gate and a SP on the L indicating the bridleway back over the top to Alwinton. You probably looked at this track climbing up the hillside as you rode up the valley. Now is your chance to sample it at close quarters.

### Kidlandlee Dean to Alwinton

You are allowed to walk the first 20 metres from the gate due to the broken nature of the track, but thereafter it is pedal power. Simply follow the track right to the top. There is a fence at the summit with a gap and a pile of stones protecting a little post bearing our blue bridleway arrow. Go SO onto the sheep-track indicated by the arrow. The going soon

***Alwinton Short Cut.*** *Most of this loop runs on wide tracks, but there is one little section high above the Alwin that is not! Matthew Barnes powering across it.*

improves to a solid path with a few technical interruptions just to test you. Eventually you reach a stile with a white-tipped post. As you cross the fence you will see the next stile 50 metres away across the field. The second stile gives you access to Clennell Street, a really ancient road, then it is down all the way to Alwinton. Do not get carried away, there are loose stones in places, and a gate hidden around the only corner. When you reach Alwinton you will have no problem finding the carpark. How about having your bait, then doing it again, in the opposite direction?

*Left: **Milfield & Coldside Hill**. Looking NW over Canno Mill up the Bowmont Water, from the elevated road near Crookhouse farm.*

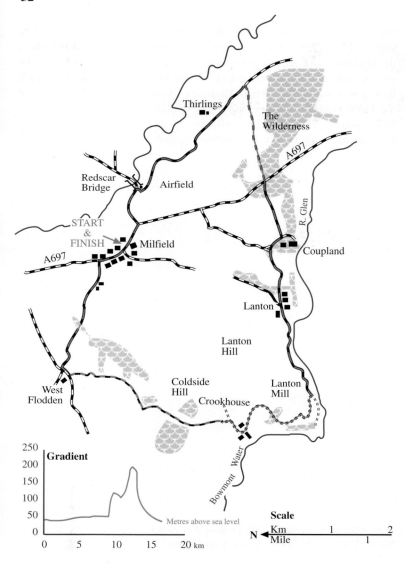

Thirlings

The Wilderness

A697

Redscar Bridge

Airfield

R. Glen

START & FINISH

Milfield

A697

Coupland

Lanton

Lanton Hill

Coldside Hill

Crookhouse

Lanton Mill

West Flodden

Bowmont Water

250
200
150
100
50
0

**Gradient**

Metres above sea level

0    5    10    15    20 km

**Scale**

N

Km    1    2

Mile    1

# 4 Milfield and Coldside Hill

| | |
|---|---|
| Grade | 16 Energetic |
| **16.5 km** | **(10.25 miles)** |
| **3.07 km** | Hill Track/Path |
| **3.45 km** | Farm/Estate Road |
| **9.98 km.** | Tarmac |
| **High Point:** | Coldside Hill 155m |
| **Maps:** | Ordnance Survey, Landranger 74 Kelso & Coldstream, Explorer 339 Kelso & Coldstream |
| **Facilities:** | Cafe and Pub in Milfield |

## PLOTTING PLAN

| *START:* | Approach | Map Reference | Depart |
|---|---|---|---|
| Milfield | – | 74/936338 | SE |
| Redscar Road End | NW | 945336$^1/_2$ | S |
| Wilderness Track | NW | 963$^1/_2$319$^1/_2$ | WSW |
| Coupland Corner | ENE | 937$^1/_2$313 | NNW |
| Lanton Mill | ENE | 911$^1/_2$307$^1/_2$ | W |
| Coldside Hill Road | SSW | 906$^1/_2$320 | N |
| West Flodden | S | 914346$^1/_2$ | NE |
| West Flodden Crossroads | SW | 915348 | SE |
| A697 | W | 933342 | SSE |
| *FINISH:* | | | |
| Milfield Country Cafe | NW | 936338 | – |

## Route Description

This is a sneaky loop: one of those routes you could take someone new to mountain biking around, con them into thinking there is nothing to it, then slap them with the difficulties when they are totally committed to doing it. There is plenty of interest if you take your time, from the ride around the perimeter track of the wartime Milfield Aerodrome (some of which is still used by the gliding club), to the alpine-style climb through the fields to Crookhouse. Late in the loop there are navigational decisions to be made, where, despite excellent definition on the map, the route on the ground has all but disappeared – a loop of considerable variety. With a little imagination you can amalgamate both this and the Ford Moss routes to give a tour exceeding 34 km worthy of anyone's attention.

## Milfield to Lanton Mill

The cafe at Milfield is a convenient starting point and their chocolate crunch is sufficient reward on your return. Depart SE then TL towards Fenton at the first opportunity. This road will take you around the northern end of the airfield. TR onto the perimeter track just before Redscar Bridge. The present road only uses half the width of the 1940s tarmac but is still unusually wide for a minor country road. Beyond the aerodrome a straight tree-lined byway takes you past Thirlings Farm before we TR onto the Wilderness track. The bridleway post announces 'Coupland' which is on our route. The wilderness has been tamed and is now a huge arable field and well-tended woodland, although the track can be a bit of a test due to its sandy composition. It is virtually level, rising only 3m in 1.3 km. However, into the teeth of a howling gale I was reduced to the lowest gear available just to make progress, and even considered walking at one point. Look for the most compacted section of the track. Take care when crossing the A697, then straight on to Coupland, (pronounced Copeland by the locals and in fact written that way in old documents). Coupland Castle is alleged to be haunted and even today there are unusual occurrences in the vicinity.

One incident involved a mechanic from Milfield Garage who decided to take a short cut through Coupland on his motor-bike that broke down near the castle. While he was repairing it he distinctly heard footsteps, looked up and passed a greeting. The footsteps went straight past him, but he saw no one. A few nights later he took the same short cut, only to suffer breakdown in the same place, and the footsteps came by again. Needless to say he has never been near the place since. Skirt the estate on its northern flank and press on to Lanton and Lanton Mill. The obelisk on Lanton Hill, which can be seen from miles around, was erected by Sir William Davidson in memory of his brother and himself!

## Lanton Mill to Milfield

It is all change at Lanton Mill. Gone are the dawdles along the riverside. You TR immediately beyond the cattle grid onto the 3-ply and it becomes a tarmac mountain bike route. Do not be frightened to stop and look about you. The effort is great, but so are the rewards. Down below the river has changed its name from the River Glen to Bowmont Water, and yet another aspect of the Cheviots reveals itself. This is real sheep country and it is not unusual to see a dozen or more tups in the field next to Crookhouse. Go SO through the farm then follow the bridleway steeply uphill on a stony road to the gate. Turn L immediately after that gate to follow the fence across to a wicket gate in the hedge. I must admit to being lured too far up the hillside to the more obvious gate in the hedge – the resultant technical ride around the lower slopes of Coldside Hill on a skinny sheep-track more than compensated for the error. As you circumnavigate Coldside Hill the sheep-track will take you to another wicket hidden among the whins (or whinnies as most Northumbrians say). Turn L slightly down to the broken wall alongside the wood. Do not he lured up to the right on what looks like a good ancient road – it does not go very far. You will see from the map that our route turns L – just beyond a little wedge-shaped wood on the R of the northern flank of Coldside Hill. Alas the wood is not there any more. Having turned through the next gate at the top of the little wood that does exist, you suddenly find a vast improvement in the track, or rather there actually is one! But it only lasts 70 metres to the next wicket. Then it is a case of following the fence again. Our bridleway status is confirmed at the next wood where a 'road' down the side of the trees is controlled by two gates. Unfortunately the field has absorbed the road again beyond the second. But the Right of Way runs down the E side of the fences so you will need to squeeze down the edge. Follow the side of the fields all the way down to the road at West Flodden. Turn R up to the XR, R again and zoom to Milfield. Hope the ghost did not get you!

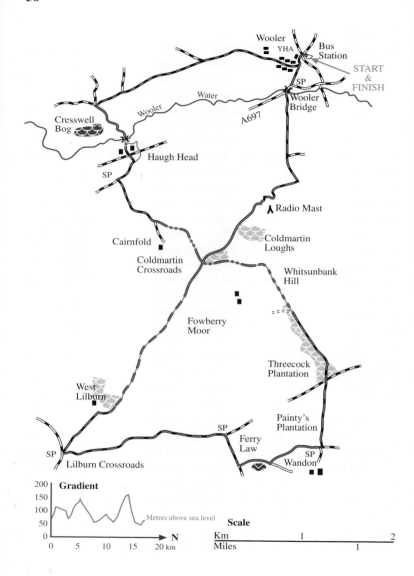

Wooler

YHA

Bus Station

START & FINISH

SP

Wooler Bridge

Water

Wooler

A697

Cresswell Bog

Haugh Head

SP

Radio Mast

Cairnfold

Coldmartin Loughs

Coldmartin Crossroads

Whitsunbank Hill

Fowberry Moor

Threecock Plantation

West Lilburn

Painty's Plantation

SP

Ferry Law

SP

Wandon

SP

Lilburn Crossroads

**Gradient**

200
150
100
50
0

Metres above sea level

0    5    10    15    20 km

**N**

**Scale**

Km                    1                    2
Miles                              1

# 5 Wooler Water & Coldmartin Loughs

| | |
|---|---|
| **Grade** | 15 Energetic |
| **16.84 km** | **(10.46 Miles)** |
| **7.11 km** | Farm Tracks/Old County Roads |
| **9.73 km** | Tarmac |
| **High Point:** | Whitsunbank Hill 167m |
| **Maps:** | Ordnance Survey, Landranger 75 Berwick upon Tweed, Explorer 340 Holy Island & Bamburgh |
| **Facilities:** | Everything in Wooler, including YHA |

## PLOTTING PLAN

| *START:* | Approach | Map Reference | Depart |
|---|---|---|---|
| Wooler Bus Station | – | 75/991$^1$/$_2$280$^1$/$_2$ | SE |
| Bog Road End | NW | 996$^1$/$_2$257 | NE |
| Cairnfold Road End | NW | 005259$^1$/$_2$ | NE |
| Coldmartin Crossroads | SW | 015269 | SE |
| Lilburn Crossroads | NW | 037$^1$/$_2$253$^1$/$_2$ | N |
| Wandon Lonnen | SW | 039274 | NW |
| Painty's Crossroads | S | 036$^1$/$_2$282$^1$/$_2$ | W |
| Threecock Plantation | E | 028$^1$/$_2$283 | W |
| Coldmartin Crossroads | N | 015269 | NW |
| *FINISH:* | | | |
| Wooler Bus Station | SE | 991$^1$/$_2$280$^1$/$_2$ | – |

## Route Description

On paper this looks quite an easy route: a high proportion of tarmac, good surfaces on old county roads and well-compacted farm tracks – motorways by moorland standards – but it is not. There are little climbs to test the best, and although route finding is relatively easy, you will learn a lot about the layout of old roads and be rewarded by views of some of the best countryside in north Northumberland. The best of these, in my opinion, is kept until last, for as you crest Whitsunbank Hill the view across the valley of Wooler Water into the Cheviots is one of my favourites. That is why the route was designed in this particular direction. We considered siting the recommended Start/Finish at Wooler Bridge, just off the A697 road, so the route would finish with the mega-downhill from the Radio Station and a whizz into Wooler, without the climb back up into the town centre. But the parking there often reaches capacity in summer, and we thought that the Bus Station was more central. There is nothing at all to stop you starting there and simply turning L into Cheviot Street at the top of the hill when you reach the Anchor Inn.

## Wooler to Lilburn Crossroads

If you stayed at the Youth Hostel you are already halfway up the hill of Cheviot Street. Otherwise you must start at the Bus Station carpark. Turn L along the main street to the Anchor, then R up Cheviot Street and out of the town. It is OK in the summer but in winter, when the legs are cold this is quite a start to the route. As you progress S, parallel to the Wooler Water you can see most of our intended route on the opposite side of the valley. Pick out the old county road we use up onto Fowberry Moor, and seek out Haugh Head on the main road in the bottom. This will help in locating our turn off at Bog Road End to take us down to the ford. Although unsurfaced and officially declared 'Unsuitable For Motor Vehicles', the run down to the river is well-used and relatively smooth. Enjoy the dash down but do not charge into the water without a careful look first. From time to time the watercourse becomes a veritable torrent, and the bridge is not just a soft option.

The A697 crossing at Haugh Head has been altered. Turn L onto the main road, then R after 40 metres and up the hill behind the cottages. After 300 metres you will see a SP way up a new concrete road. The old road has been surfaced, I suspect by the owners of the new house at the top – and what appears on the map as an old track turns out to be a lot easier than expected. However, it does not go all the way. At the last corner before the house, we go SO through the blue gate, then the red gate and up the side of the fields. The climb is sustained and the uneven surface can make it a bit of a test. On the ridge there is a conglomeration

***Wooler Water & Coldmartin Loughs.*** *Crossing the Wooler Water is the lowest part of the route, but in winter you may be best advised to do a 'Williams' and ride across the bridge. A feat demanding concentration, poise and bottle!*

of gates. The best advice is to go more or less SO and keep the exit wall on your L. Then choose the best rut! Coldmartin Crossroads lie at the far side of the field right next to the trees. This is the centre of our figure of eight loop, and once you reach there all the hard work is done! TR down the stony lonnen, out into the open fields. Follow the track along the ridge all the way to the beautiful wooden house at West Lilburn and down to Lilburn Crossroads.

## Lilburn Crossroads to Wooler

Turning very sharp L takes us towards Chatton. Bear R with the main road at Ferny Law, then slot L onto another old county road towards Wandon. Our route bears L at the end of the duckpond and becomes a little rougher – but you should not go wrong. The discreet 'Private' sign on one of the old stone gateposts should catch your eye. The descent to the XR at the end of Painty's Plantation is a bit bumpy, so bear with the novices in your company. Or if you are a novice, keep off the front brake! Turn L at the XR and, as you toil up to the next XR at Threecock Plantation take note of the interesting stone walling. Then beyond the XR note how the style changes and the stones are much larger. The tarmac veers L into the private road to Fowberry Moor Farm. But we go SO to Whitsunbank Hill, the highest point on the route. Then it is down to Coldmartin Crossroads again, R along past the Loughs and downhill in a major way from the Radio Station when you will be able to freewheel all the way to the A697. If you parked in the town centre it is only 300 metres to the top of the hill.

*Left: Greensheen Hill. Final stages of the ride beneath the summit of Greensheen Hill, heading towards Holborn, but if you use the Holburn Grange carpark it will be one of the first.*

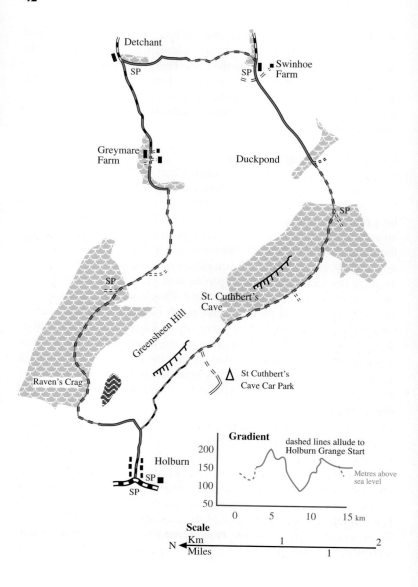

Detchant

SP

SP ▪ Swinhoe Farm

Greymare Farm ▪ ▪

Duckpond

SP

SP

St. Cuthbert's Cave

Greensheen Hill

Raven's Crag

△ St Cuthbert's Cave Car Park

Holburn

SP ▪

SP

**Gradient** dashed lines allude to Holburn Grange Start

200

150

100

50

0        5        10        15 km

Metres above sea level

**Scale**

N ◄ Km —————————— 1 —————————— 2

Miles —————————— 1

# 6 Circuit of Greensheen Hill

| | |
|---|---|
| **Grade** | 15 Energetic |
| **12.61 km** | **(7.84 Miles)** |
| **3.21 km** | Forest/Moorland Track |
| **7.48 km** | Farm/Estate Road |
| **1.92 km** | Tarmac |
| **High Points:** | Ravens Crag 154m, St. Cuthberts Cave 152m |
| **Maps:** | Ordnance Survey, Landranger 75 Berwick upon Tweed, Explorer 340 Holy Island & Bamburgh |
| **Facilities:** | None. Be self-sufficient |

## PLOTTING PLAN

| *START:* | Approach | Map Reference | Depart |
|---|---|---|---|
| Holburn | – | 041362 | E |
| Raven's Crag | WNW | 050367 | E |
| Greymare Farm | W | 073361 | E |
| Detchant | SW | 084$\frac{1}{2}$364$\frac{1}{2}$ | S |
| Swinhoe Farm | E | 083$\frac{1}{2}$350$\frac{1}{2}$ | SW |
| Near St. Cuthbert's Cave | SSE | 058351 | NNW |
| Holburn Road | SE | 045$\frac{1}{2}$361 | W |
| *FINISH:* | | | |
| Holburn | E | 041362 | – |

## Route Description

This is a supreme family route: mainly well-surfaced, blessed with gradual climbs and the views are great. To the W one looks across to the Cheviots and their northern outliers, then after crossing the watershed, probably the best view from anywhere of Holy Island and the Farnes presents itself. There is a bit of a challenge on the bridleway between Detchant and Swinhoe late in summer due to metre-high weeds – but you cannot expect it to be easy all the way, and it is only 200 metres! There is now a small carpark for Cuthbert's Cave at Holburn Grange, map ref. 651 351$\frac{1}{2}$. If chosen, follow the farm-track bridleway NE then turn L to join the route below the crags of Greensheen Hill.

## Holburn to Detchant

Holburn is a working farm. Park with obvious consideration, or even a little way from the hamlet and ride in to start the route. Ride E through the farm as directed by the SP pointing the way to Greymare Farm and Detchant. This is where we are going. Follow the main track around to the N as it climbs towards the forest. It will be obvious that this first kilometre is well-used by farm traffic, but as you enter the wood the surface changes. There is still a firm, stony base but for most of the way through the wood you will need to choose the best rut. Sadly, Small Lake now hosts the finest selection of rushes and reeds in North Northumberland, and only in the depths of the wettest winter will it resemble anything like a sheet of water. As you near the edge of the forest, look hard at the trees. There was a serious fire here in 1990 and many of the trees still have blackened trunks. Much of the ground is deep peat which smouldered for weeks. But surely a warning with regard to fires is superfluous to serious mountain bikers. Out onto the moor the incredible view across to Lindisfarne reveals itself. One grey September morning while checking this route, the sea was so still there was practically a mirror image of the castle in the sheltered waters of Fenham Flats. Unfortunately I did not have a telephoto lens to record the moment; one of those images one just has to commit to memory. I hope you see the same.

The descent to Greymare Farm is a bit stony, the middle grass being the best option. Then there is a 50-kph tarmac hurtle down to Detchant. Turn R onto another stony track at the L-hand bend before reaching the first houses of Detchant. There is a SP hidden in the hedge on the R at the end of the track. You will probably not see it until you have stopped.

## Detchant to Holburn

The Swinhoe bridleway becomes a field road then a mere path along the hedge. It is so overgrown in late summer that you will probably doubt if a track exists at all. Have faith, keep going until you reach a gate on the L, then go through it. All the other 'gates' are simply openings. This is one place where a computer will be invaluable. Having gone through the gate, keep close to the fence on the L, on the path of the old raised road. In due course you will bridge the road to Swinhoe Farm. When the tarmac ends in Swinhoe there are many signs. Follow the good farm road towards Dick's Oldwalls and Holburn. Just over a kilometre later there is a junction. Go through the gate and up the side of the field on an old green track again. Pause and investigate the duckpond just out of sight on the R. I would be surprised if you do not see more mallard than you have ever seen before. The wettest part of the route awaits. Follow the track around to the R in the wood and look for the best line. There is only a couple of hundred metres where it is squelchy but it can be a bit of a test before it exits onto the side of the hill. It is gently downhill all the way from here with great views of the Cheviots and the unexpected treat of St. Cuthbert's Cave. It is amazing how big it is and the hewn graffiti is historic. The notice at the far end of the wood reads: *This natural sandstone cave is said to have been one of the resting places for the body of St. Cuthbert on its journey from Lindisfarne to Durham Cathedral in the eleventh century.*

The final stanza is a moorland ride on a track of ever diminishing proportions, ending up as a sheep-track across the edge of the field to rejoin the farm road to Holburn. Do not forget to leave the gates as you find them. Thanks.

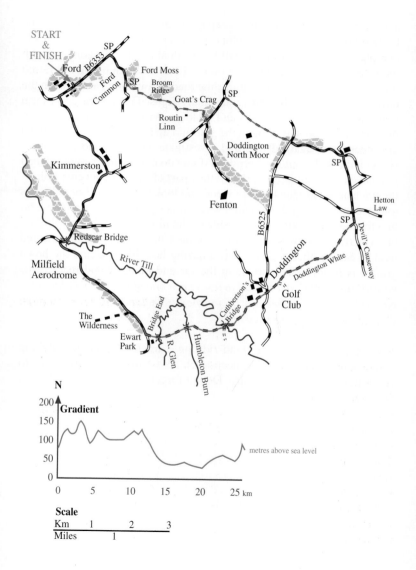

START & FINISH

Ford B6353 SP

Ford Moss

Ford Common

Broom Ridge

Goat's Crag SP

Routin Linn

Doddington North Moor

Kimmerston

Fenton

B6525

SP

Hetton Law

SP

Devil's Causeway

Redscar Bridge

River Till

Milfield Aerodrome

Doddington

Cuthbertson's Bridge

Doddington White

Golf Club

The Wilderness

Bridge End

Ewart Park

R. Glen

Humbleton Burn

**Gradient**

N

200
150
100
50
0

metres above sea level

0    5    10    15    20    25 km

**Scale**

Km    1    2    3

Miles    1

# 7 Ford Moss & Doddington

| | |
|---|---|
| **Grade** | 13 Energetic |
| **25.27 km** | **(15.7 Miles)** |
| **3.9 km** | Moorland and Lesser Tracks |
| **0.32 km** | Forest Track |
| **5.19 km** | Farm/Estate Road |
| **15.81 km** | Tarmac |
| **High Point:** | Broom Ridge 151m |
| **Maps:** | Ordnance Survey, Landranger 75 Berwick-upon-Tweed, Explorers 339 Kelso & Coldstream, 340 Holy Island & Bamburgh. |
| **Facilities:** | Cafe in Ford |

## PLOTTING PLAN

| *START:* | Approach | Map Reference | Depart |
|---|---|---|---|
| Horseshoe Smithy, Ford | – | 75/948376$^1/_2$ | S |
| B6353 | SW | 958383 | SE |
| Ford Moss | NW | 964$^1/_2$375 | SE |
| Routin Linn Road End | NNW | 983$^1/_2$366$^1/_2$ | NE |
| Bar Moor | SSW | 989$^1/_2$375$^1/_2$ | SE |
| Doddington North Moor Bridge | NW | 006362 | SE |
| Hetton Law Crossroads | NNW | 021$^1/_2$344 | SSE |
| Doddington White | NNW | 022341 | SW |
| DODDINGTON | NE | 999324 | SW |
| Bridge End | ESE | 968314 | NW |
| Redscar Bridge | S | 945336$^1/_2$ | ENE |
| Kimmerston | SW | 957$^1/_2$353$^1/_2$ | NW |
| Ford, B6353 | SE | 944$^1/_2$372$^1/_2$ | NE |
| *FINISH:* | | | |
| Horsehoe Smithy | S | 948376$^1/_2$ | – |

## Route Description

It has its moments! This is probably the most varied route in the guide. If you tried to put so many different types of terrain together on purpose, you would probably tear your hair out trying to do it – but it just fell this way. And if you add the Milfield & Coldside Hill loop to it, not only will you manufacture a substantial day out, but also a little of everything Northumberland has to offer with the exception of altitude. None of the route is too technical but there is a little stretch up onto Broom Ridge that will test you; and the section from the E side of Fenton Wood across Doddington North Moor involves a bit of navigation because the bridleway has all but disappeared.

## Horseshoe Smithy to Hetton Law Crossroads

Most smithies shoe horses; this one has the architecture to match. You will see when you get there! Depart S back to the B6353. TL at the junction and climb steadily onto Ford Common where we TR towards Kimmerston. Bear L onto an unsurfaced track at the end of a little wood and follow the sign for 'Roughting Linn'. This is the poshest spelling for Routin Lynn I have ever seen, but it points the right way nevertheless.

A gentle climb takes you around to Ford Moss Nature Reserve with its striking chimney. This was the flue of a steam engine which pumped water out of the coal workings many years ago – the only clue to the fact that this was an industrial site. We skirt the Moss on its southern flank, gently climbing up onto Broom Ridge on the old bridleway. As you will see there is more than one route heading for Goats Crag. But they all converge before you get there. TR immediately through the gate and zoom down and round to Routin Lynn. Climbers are banned from the crag from the 1st March to May to allow birds to nest in peace. I ask that you pass quietly by at this time and afford them the same respect. Thank you. When you reach the tarmac at Routin Lynn XR TL up the hill, out onto the open moor again and look out for the bridleway SP at the top of the hill. The fingerpost points the way to Doddington North Moor Bridge, but the sign on the gate says 'Beware of the Bull'. The track is not much more welcoming – it is good initially but becomes somewhat vague as you cross the moor. Keep aiming towards the bridge which is in the far dip, virtually surrounded by trees. Keep well R of the stream. When you reach the B6525 go 'straight across' towards the Hettons. TR at the next XR towards the Hortons, and follow this old Roman road, the Devil's Causeway all the way to Hetton Law XR.

## Hetton Law Crossroads to Bridge End

300 metres beyond the XR TR onto 3-ply, in the dip affectionately known in the motor-rallying fraternity as The Doddington White. This is an old county road that was never fully surfaced and nowadays provides a great off-road ride, especially in this direction. You will cross some of the fattest cattle grids in the country before you reach Doddington, and with a bit of luck the sole gate will be open. Take care as you reach the tarmac near Wooler Golf Club – no one expects a flying mountain biker leaping over the cattle grid! A little caution is needed again as you negotiate the offset XR in Doddington – then follow the sign for Bridge End. There are actually three bridges to cross. The first is Cuthbertson's Bridge over the River Till which is approaching 200 years old and showing signs of wear.

A pause on the arch will let you see how much the Till rises and falls; and it is a good vantage point from which to view the levee flood-control embankments, which, as you will see as soon as you TR through the gate, have become the farmers' roads. Sadly, we do not get to use the elevated twin track. Our Right of Way goes through the rusty gate on the L after 150 metres and follows the side of the field. It then crosses the levee again and heads for the tiny brick bridge over the Humbleton Burn beneath the pylons.

Follow the hedge along a good green road to Bridge End. But just before you get there, the last levee takes you onto Ewart Park Bridge, built privately in 1799 by Colonel, Count Horace St. Paul. After crossing the River Glen you feel that you are riding on an elevated road but in fact this is still the bridge. There are a total of 14 flood arches, then a secondary trestle bridge which was repaired in 1991/92, before you reach the buildings.

## Bridge End to Ford

The tarmac TJ at Ewart Park marks the end of off-road; unless you TL onto Wilderness track 0.69 km up the road to add the Milfield loop. The run past the old Milfield Aerodrome gets the legs back into a good pedalling rhythm. TR across the Redscar Bridge and twiddle up to Kimmerston where we TL just beyond the telephone kiosk for the pleasant run to Ford. Whereas most routes in this guide have a downhill to finish with, this one has a horrendous climb back up through the village to the smithy. Sorry – but you can always walk and admire the castle, the school, and arguably the best village architecture in Northumberland.

*Right: Ford Moss & Doddington. Neil Welsh, the first to ride all the routes in the original edition. Now he has another eight to do, but we know for a fact that he tasted some bits many moons ago.*

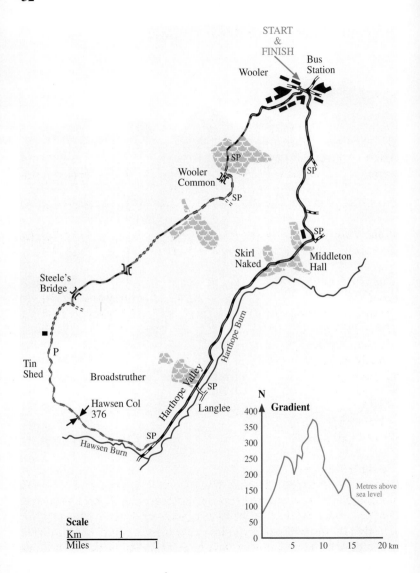

START & FINISH

Wooler

Bus Station

SP

Wooler Common

SP

SP

SP

Skirl Naked

Middleton Hall

Steele's Bridge

Tin Shed

P

Broadstruther

Harthope Burn

Hawsen Col 376

Harthope Valley

SP

Langlee

SP

Hawsen Burn

N

Gradient

400
350
300
250
200
150
100
50
0

Metres above sea level

5        10        15        20 km

Scale

Km                    1
Miles                    1

# 8 Wooler Common & Broadstruther

| | |
|---|---|
| **Grade** | 20 Strenuous |
| **17.26 km** | **(10.72 Miles)** |
| **7.5 km** | Moorland Track/Path |
| **0.47 km** | Forest Track/Path |
| **0.16 km** | Farm/Estate Road |
| **9.13 km** | Tarmac |
| **High Point:** | Hawsen Col 376m |
| **Maps:** | Ordnance Survey, Landranger 75 Berwick-upon-Tweed, Explorer OL16 Cheviot Hills |
| **Facilities:** | Everything you want in Wooler, including Youth Hostel |

*Note: This route can be extended by amalgamating with the Langlee Crags loop, producing a Grade 23 tour*

## PLOTTING PLAN

| *START:* | Approach | Map Reference | Depart |
|---|---|---|---|
| Wooler Bus Station | – | 75/991280$^1$/$_2$ | WSW |
| Brown's Law | NE | 976$^1$/$_2$272 | SSW |
| Wooler Common | E | 973265 | WSW |
| Broadstruther | NNE | 941249 | SSW |
| Hawsen Col | NW | 944$^1$/$_2$232 | SE |
| Harthope Valley | W | 955226 | NE |
| Middleton Hall | WSW | 988$^1$/$_2$255 | NNW |
| *FINISH:* | | | |
| Wooler Bus Station | SE | 991280$^1$/$_2$ | – |

## Route Description

Despite its length and grading, this route can become a very serious undertaking if the weather deteriorates, or there is a wind of any strength. The prevailing westerly seems to be channelled and intensified by The Cheviot, resulting in some hellish gusts in the vicinity of Broadstruther. On more than one occasion we have been blown off the track. The route is difficult enough without the embellishment of a gale in your face, and should you arrive at Wooler only to be confronted by strong winds, you would be well-advised to think again, and perhaps consider the Bewick Moor route some 10.5 km to the SE. This route is about 100m lower and you will have the wind behind you as you climb. Having said all of this, there are many spots where you can sit and enjoy the countryside on route 8. On a sunny day you could become addicted to it, plus there are a few stretches that will test your technique to the limit.

**Wooler to Broadstruther**

Ramsey's Lane rises WSW from the very centre of Wooler, and goes on climbing with little respite for nearly 1 km. Then there is a slight downhill to the little bridge near Brown's Law where we fork L onto the bridleway to Wooler Common and Broadstruther. The pattern is set. Climb, then a little bit down, climb more then lose a bit, but ever higher. Following the SP for Wooler Common takes you to a gate, and beyond onto a steep, stony track. The track eases, becomes more grassy, and eventually brings you to the junction with the farm road to Wooler Common Farm. The SP says Hell Path which could allude to any stretch of the route in bad weather, but I hope your journey is more of a heavenly nature. TR along to the farm then follow the obvious farm road L and R around the red shed. Strictly speaking the bridleway goes around the other side of the farm, to come out at the same place – but it seems only sensible to use the well-worn road. Aim for the gap between the woods on the skyline. Keep to the S side of the broken wall and you cannot go wrong. When the woods end go SO across the moor with the vehicle tracks which will bring you to the edge of another forest. The stile gives you access to an exciting bit of downhill. TR at the bottom onto a lumpy path alongside the Carey Burn. A blue arrow confirms the route.

Take care on the little wooden bridge in damp conditions, it can be very slippy. A short carry will be necessary away from the burn, but fortunately the bank side is on your L so you should not be impeded. Follow the path high above the burn until you reach the new 'Steele's' bridge. Cross the bridge then join the obvious track that leads up to Broadstruther. Pick the best rut!

## Broadstruther to Langlee

Broadstruther is now only a fodder store, but a great place to eat. No, not the hay! The view from the front doorstep is terrific. The obvious road beyond the paddock will lure you too high. The bridleway uses the stile at the junction of the fences in front of the house, then crosses the field to a knackered gate. Then you really need to look well ahead to follow the track. It is all there and all rideable, apart from the odd ditch, but it will improve your moorcraft considerably! Confirmation is provided by a large post and a concrete pad, which could have been the base of a building, then a large stone near the tin shed. Thereafter, it is a case of following the best sheep-track and aiming for the gate on the col visible on the skyline. You should strike a good track as you rise out of the bowl towards the col. If you should stray, just follow the fence until you reach the gate at the lowest point, and reorientate there.

The terrain changes as soon as you reach Hawsen Col. You enter an area of steep sided valleys and an exciting descent to the Harthope Burn. Keep L and keep high above Hawsen Bum when you have the choice. Do not be tempted by the track on the opposite side of the valley. The tarmac road comes all too soon. TL and follow the road downstream until you reach Middleton Hall. The option to extend the route arrives after 0.92 km on the tarmac road when you can TR across the river to Langlee and follow the Langlee Crags route to Threestone Burn and beyond. It might be an idea to do both routes individually and then come back another day (when the weather is right) and go for the big one.

## Langlee to Wooler

I really enjoy the ride down the valley, but the horrendous little hill at Skirl Naked comes as a nasty surprise. Fortunately it is on the S facing slope and is not too prone to ice in winter – but watch out for the Sunday motorists lurching over the top in summer. There is a SP for Wooler at Middleton Hall, then it is plain sailing all the way to the finish.

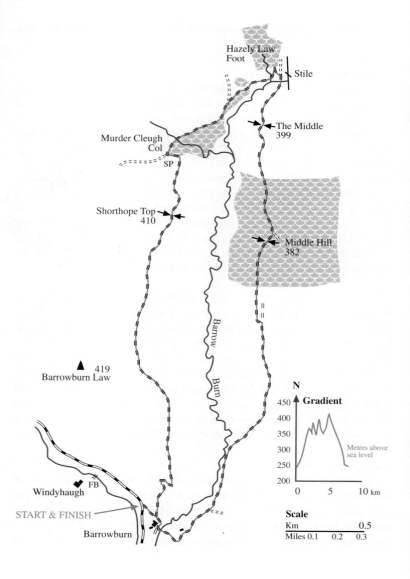

Hazely Law
Foot

Stile

The Middle
399

Murder Cleugh
Col

SP

Shorthope Top
410

Middle Hill
382

Barrow

Burn

▲ 419
Barrowburn Law

Windyhaugh

FB

START & FINISH

Barrowburn

N

**Gradient**

Metres above
sea level

0        5        10 km

**Scale**

Km                          0.5
Miles  0.1    0.2    0.3

# 9 Barrowburn Loop

| | |
|---|---|
| **Grade** | 18 Strenuous |
| **7.53 km** | **(4.68 Miles)** |
| **5.8 km** | Moorland Track |
| **1.34 km** | Forest Road |
| **0.39 km** | Farm Road |

**High Points:** Middle Hill 382m, The Middle 399m, Shorthope Top 410m

**Maps:** Ordnance Survey, Landranger 80, Cheviot Hills & Kielder Water Area, Explorer OL16 Cheviot Hills

**Facilities:** None. Although short, this is a pure moorland route.

## PLOTTING PLAN

| *START:* | Approach | Map Reference | Depart |
|---|---|---|---|
| Windyhaugh | – | 80/866109¹/₂ | SE |
| Barrowburn | NW | 868107 | SE |
| Middle Hill | SSW | 874¹/₂126 | N |
| Hazely Law Foot | S | 875137 | SW |
| Murder Cleugh Head | NE | 867¹/₂132 | SE |
| Barrow Law | NW | 867117 | SE |
| Barrowburn | N | 867108 | NW |
| *FINISH:* | | | |
| Windyhaugh | SE | 866109¹/₂ | – |

## Route Description

This little loop is pure off-road, no tarmac at all. Both fords have concrete bottoms, but they are usually so slippy that it does not count. I must admit that I had never ridden this route until I covered it for the guide. I have been above it, below it, used bits of it as access to greater things, and now regret having neglected it for so long. Rewarding, strength-sapping in places, it is all rideable if you are fit enough, but if you do not dismount at least once I would be surprised. It has become a test piece with the Simonside Snipes. If you can ride this all the way round, you are fit enough to race. I will never be! There is a little loose section just over a kilometre from the start that ALWAYS has me off. See how you fare. You will recognise it when you get there.

## Windyhaugh to Hazely Law Foot

There is good parking at the side of the road just beyond Barrowburn, near the footbridge to Windyhaugh Farm. The official Start is 50 metres back down the road, at the corner where you can go through a gate onto a 3-ply farm road that will take you to the back of Barrowburn. This is our route. Follow this track to Barrowburn, then through the ford behind the buildings and up to the corner where the road turns L through a gate. Jink R past the end of a wooden building and you are on your way. The road climbs a little more, drops down to the burn again, then up the far side. You will see it all laid out before you. After you splash through the puddles in the bottom, hit the low gears and think positive. It is not far and it is a beautiful surface. The view will be great when you get to the top. From the gate into the forestry at the top the scenery is magnificent. You are on a ridge separating two valleys and you can see down both. (Route 18 uses the one to the E from Fairhaugh which you can see just below you to Batailshiel Haugh which is hidden around the corner). Immediately through this gate into the forest, jink L and R onto the higher and grassier of the two forest roads. Keep maximum speed and force it to the top of Middle Hill. Just over the top the road becomes very rutted and muddy, a bit of a test. Stay with this track as it bears slightly L and down to the gate at the edge of the wood. More concentration, effort and positive thinking are now required for the next climb onto The Middle. Again it is possible, unless it is extremely wet, and the view from the top is different again. Our route uses the old green road N of the trees on the far side of the burn. Note where it lies, it will help you after we TL beyond the gate at the bottom. If it is wet do not howl down off the summit, the gate is nearer than it looks!

## Hazely Law Foot to Barrowburn

80 metres beyond the gate TL down the zigzag to the burn, opposite the little stile on the R. Watch the approach to the ford if you are doing a

**Barrowburn Loop.** *Barrowburn, Upper Coquetdale, with the final downhill finish clearly visible from the skyline behind the farm.*

winter circuit. This is a favourite sheltering place for the sheep and the last 20 metres to the ford can often be like a skating rink as a result. We did it only two or three days after the snow had melted. Alex Spence lost it on the approach, slid a lot further than he might have wished, then flipped over the edge of the track and stopped with one foot in the water. Then, to add insult to injury no one would sit beside him at bait time! At the top of the green track you join the 'main' shale road. TL and climb up through the trees to Murder Cleugh col. We TL through a gate at the end of the trees on the L, at a SP for Barrowburn. Once through the gate bear R onto the most obvious track. Follow this over Shorthope Top all the way back to Barrowburn. It is an impressive ride in wide, open space and the final descent to the farm is great. Do not go too fast or your eyes might drop out!

*Left: Langlee Crags. Bright sunshine, snow showers, lots of sweat and wet underfoot. Typical of the Cheviots. Alex Spence, well versed with the terrain kitted out with breathable top and gaiters on the climb past Langlee Crags.*

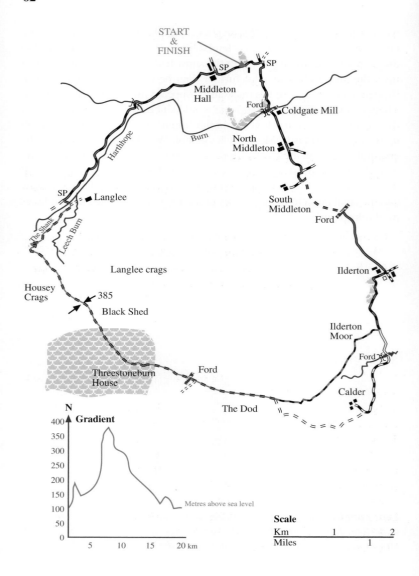

START & FINISH

SP

Middleton Hall

SP

Ford

Coldgate Mill

North Middleton

Burn

Harthope

SP

Langlee

The Shank

Leech Burn

Langlee crags

South Middleton

Ford

Ilderton

Housey Crags

385

Black Shed

Ilderton Moor

Ford

Threestoneburn House

Ford

Calder

The Dod

**N**

400
350
300
250
200
150
100
50
0

**Gradient**

5      10      15      20 km

Metres above sea level

**Scale**

| Km | 1 | 2 |
| Miles | 1 | |

# 10 Langlee Crags & Threestoneburn

| | |
|---|---|
| **Grade** | 20 Strenuous |
| **19.26 km** | **(11.97 Miles)** |
| **5.48 km** | Moorland Track/Path |
| **1.15 km** | Forest Track/Path |
| **4.51 km** | Farm Road |
| **8.12 km** | Tarmac |
| **High Point:** | Langlee Crags 385m |
| **Maps:** | Ordnance Survey, Landrangers 75 Berwick upon Tweed, & 81 Alnwick & Morpeth, Explorer OL16 Cheviot hills |
| **Facilities:** | Water/Toilets at Middleton Hall Picnic Area. |

*Comment: This route can be extended by amalgamating with the Wooler & Broadstruther loop, then producing a Grade 23 tour. Lambing comes late on these high moors. Please avoid this route between mid April and mid May.*

## PLOTTING PLAN

| *START:* | Approach | Map Reference | Depart |
|---|---|---|---|
| Middleton Hall Picnic Area | – | 75/994256 | WSW |
| Langlee | NE | 963233 | SW |
| Langlee Crags Col | NNW | 964216 | SE |
| Threestoneburn House | NW | 975204 | ESE |
| The Dod | W | 81/992199 | E |
| Power Pole | SW | 003$\frac{1}{2}$197$\frac{1}{2}$ | ENE |
| Ilderton Moor | WSW | 75/015$\frac{1}{2}$209$\frac{1}{2}$ | NNW |
| Ilderton crossroads | SW | 016$\frac{1}{2}$219$\frac{1}{2}$ | NW |
| Coldgate Mill Ford | SSE | 997$\frac{1}{2}$248$\frac{1}{2}$ | N |
| *FINISH:* | | | |
| Middleton Hall Picnic Area | E | 994256 | – |

## Route Description

This is one of those routes it is best not to do if it is wet, or if there has been prolonged rain in the preceding days. The track from Langlee over the col between the crags and on to Threestoneburn House really does not like water. In particular, the kilometre from the end of the wall to the Black Shed is set on peat, and unless the shepherd's landrover has compacted it for you very recently, it can be quite a fight. Having said all of this, there is a fair percentage of tarmac, some excellent, hard-packed, fast farm road and a good stretch of old county road; but it is the moorland that makes the route. A further consideration can be the amalgamation of this route with the Wooler Common loop to give a substantial day out. I recommend starting at Wooler Bus Station if you do, and that way you will avoid the horrendous little tarmac climb at Skirl Naked. It always kills me!

## Middleton to Threestoneburn House

You can fill your water bottles at the Middleton Hall Picnic Area, and there is ample parking. TL out of the carpark along to Middleton Hall, then TL again up the hill towards Langleeford. Apologies about the hill so early in the route. Is it because it is so early after you set off and you are not fully warmed up, or is it really one of the steepest bits of tarmac in the county? The OS map gives it two arrows to denote a gradient '1 in 5 or steeper', then a second single arrow 100m further up denoting '1 in 7 to 1 in 5 – it is awful. Sorry. But what it does do is give you access to one of the most beautiful valleys in Northumberland, and the run alongside the Harthope Burn is interesting at any time of year.

Quit the tarmac at Langlee. There are SPs for Threestoneburn House, both as you leave the road, then near the track at the far side of the bridge. You do not need to go along to Langlee itself. Once through the gate keep close to the fence. Then bear L along the top of The Shank keeping the little Leech Burn on your L. You should be able to see the faint impression of the old track climbing up the ever steepening hillside. Make a mental note of the route because the view diminishes as you climb. However, the track becomes more distinct, being set a metre or so lower than the surrounding moor, particularly near the top in the zigzags. One minor warning: the little stream crossing 100 metres beyond the valley floor looks rideable but is usually several centimetres deep in granite sand. Really blitz it and you might just get through. If not be prepared to hop off. When you reach the wall at the top, TL and follow it until it ends. The sheep-track weaves its way through stones and little boulders but is all rideable with a bit of trail craft. Immediately the wall ends there is a gate at a culvert over a stream. Go R through it, then 20 metres across the heather and L onto what looks like a boggy firebreak across the moor. This is our track. If you are using the Explorer map you will see that it gradually drifts away from the fence, but is well-defined. It is important to use the gate to get onto the track because, apart from the chance of damaging the fence, if you follow the posts you will never see the track hidden in the heather.

Langlee Crags are on your L, Housey and Long Crags away on your R. The great cone of Hedgehope dominates the western skyline. It is quite an effort to get up here but the feeling of space is terrific and the views are great. The riding is not bad either. The col, 385m, is quite flat. Then, as you start to descend, look for the Black Shed. It is only a fodder store but the best landmark around. A good place to have your banana if you like a woolly audience. The sheep well know what the shed contains and always come to see you in the hope of easy food. Aim for the wicket gate into the forestry then follow the gap through the trees towards Threestoneburn. The tussocks and lack of any semblance of regular use make the bridleway one of the ultimate challenges. But because it is downhill you will just about make it to the wall of the enclosure without more than three or four dismounts. Threestoneburn House is the farm across the paddock. Follow the path which automatically leads you to the bridges. Then weave your way through the farm, with the appropriate consideration please.

### Threestoneburn House to Middleton

The road from Threestoneburn House is typical forestry track, but the trees end a short distance E of the old farm and you are out on the moor again. Simply follow this good, hard-packed road down past The Dod. Then bear L onto a little moorland path immediately beyond the first cattle grid. Initially power poles run parallel with the path and the fence, leading you across the Harelaw Burn at a tiny ford that always seems to attract more standing water than is reasonable. Climb up to the gate. Bear L immediately after the gate, up under the power lines, then TR onto a Quad track at the first opportunity. This will take you around to a little wood where it is best to keep high. Choose the best track worn by the shepherd. Contour around the hill actually climbing slightly at one point. Then aim for Ilderton Moor, protected by the trees. The descent is great. Good, grassy track with enough undulations to entertain anyone. Keep your eye out for the peacocks at the farm then TL when you reach the road. The tarmac takes you around to the XR at Ilderton. TL onto an old county road which hosts a ford with the added attraction of no alternative bridge! It is several metres wide, usually quite shallow, but loose and stony on the bottom. You are bound to lose traction on the mobile base so try to enter as fast as you can, and hope that frantic pedalling and a death grip on the handlebars will get you through. Even then it is only semi-successful because you will become quite wet. Take heart, it is not far to the finish, and you can blast the last ford at Coldgate Mill and not even bother to stay dry! When you reach the tarmac again TR downhill, then TL at the first opportunity towards Middleton. Coldgate Mill ford comes next – heed the depth boards, and there is a bridge upstream this time. Continue along to the oddly-shaped XR where the SP points the way to Middleton and the finish. If you have done this section as the second part of the amalgamated loop, go SO at the XR and follow your nose to Wooler.

*Right: Bewick Moor. Calm and frozen solid on Bewick Moor. Ideal conditions. Anything else, wait for summer!*

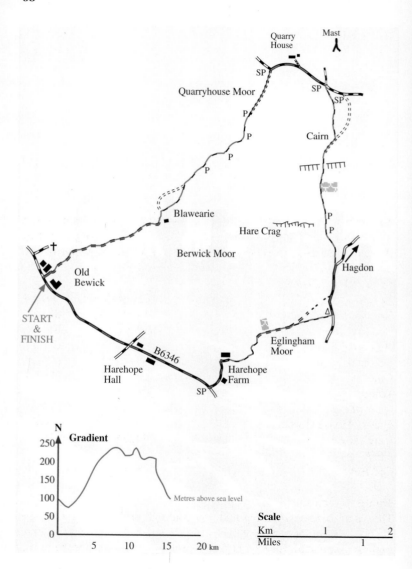

Quarry House

Mast ʎ

SP

Quarryhouse Moor

SP

SP

P

P

Cairn

P

P

ᴛᴛᴛᴛ   ᴛᴛᴛᴛ

P

Blawearie

Hare Crag   ᴛᴛᴛ

P

Berwick Moor   P

† Hagdon

Old Bewick

START & FINISH

Harehope Hall

B6346

Harehope Farm

SP

Eglingham Moor

N

**Gradient**

250
200
150
100
50
0

Metres above sea level

5   10   15   20 km

**Scale**

Km                1                2

Miles                      1

# 11 Bewick Moor

| | |
|---|---|
| **Grade** | 20 Strenuous |
| **15.7 km** | **(9.74 Miles)** |
| **9.6 km** | Moorland Track/Path |
| **1.27 km** | Farm/Estate Road |
| **4.8 km** | Tarmac |
| **High Point:** | Cairn, Quarryhouse Moor 234m |
| **Maps:** | Ordnance Survey, Landranger 75 Berwick upon Tweed, Explorers 332 Alnwick & Amble, 340 Holy Island & Bamburgh |

*Comment: Moorland Plateau route. Very little shelter. Go prepared. Avoid this route altogether between mid April and the beginning of June to allow the grouse to nest and hatch undisturbed. Thank you.*

## PLOTTING PLAN

| *START:* | Approach | Map Reference | Depart |
|---|---|---|---|
| Old Bewick | – | 75/066215 | SE |
| B6346 | NW | 089201 | SE |
| Harehope Farm | S | 093$\frac{1}{2}$203 | E |
| Eglingham Moor | WSW | 110$\frac{1}{2}$209$\frac{1}{2}$ | N |
| Gate | S | 110$\frac{1}{2}$217 | N |
| Wood | S | 108$\frac{1}{2}$227 | N |
| Quarryhouse Moor | SE | 109243$\frac{1}{2}$ | NW |
| Quarry House Corner | NE | 100$\frac{1}{2}$245$\frac{1}{2}$ | SSW |
| Blawearie | N | 084224 | SW |
| *FINISH:* | | | |
| Old Bewick | NE | 066215 | – |

## Route Description

This route is so entertaining that you could go back tomorrow, do it in the opposite direction and see just as much again. And probably feel the same sense of achievement, although nothing quite matches the reward one feels having successfully negotiated a bit of difficult terrain for the first time. If I was forced to nominate one route from this guide, and one route only, that sums up Northumbrian mountain biking at its best, this loop would probably win. It is splendidly situated giving extensive views of the Farne Islands and the north Northumbrian coastline on the outward leg. Then, when you run for home, you have arguably the finest views of the Cheviot Hills from any quarter. Coupled to this the terrain is very technical in places, and temptations to stray from the official route abound. In fact if your distances tally exactly with mine on the moorland stretches, I will be most surprised. You will be reduced to walking a couple of times, but do not be put off. These are minor impediments.

## Old Bewick to Quarry House

There is some space available for parking at Old Bewick, but bear in mind that this is a big busy farm. Do not obstruct the roads or risk having your vehicle scratched by a huge agricultural machine. I usually do an extra 400 metres and park at the chapel road end alongside the Kirk Burn to prevent any problems. Follow the main road (B 6346) SE past Harehope Hall, then TL up the hill to Harehope Farm. The SP will keep you right. Go past the farmhouse then TR down the front of the cottages and you are on your way. Initially the fields look very cultivated, and they certainly are well-kept. A blue bridleway arrow at the first gate will confirm the route for you. Then it is a case of following the track to the next gate and across the field to the stream. The official bridleway shows a ford crossing, but now there is a bridge. It seems only sensible to use this. Beyond the bridge follow the track as it climbs up the hill with the wall. It winds its way past the wood on the L, and across the moor. Just opposite the wood a well-defined track used to join our thoroughfare. But the size of the gate through the wall now restricts access to smaller vehicles and horses, so the junction has virtually disappeared.

Follow the obvious track as it climbs again, but this is where we start to wander. Modern usage has moved the track a few metres further N than the designated line. By the time you reach the farm road that leads to

Hagdon, you will probably have drifted N of the triangulation pillar, and will actually join it a lot nearer the gate than you intended. It does not matter. Simply re-orientate at the gate then head N for the wood, up the E side of the wall. There is very little trace of the old bridleway between here and Quarry House. You can clearly see the line it took to the E of Hare Crag, then immediately W of the wood, and virtually due N to the radio masts – but finding a rideable line is a major challenge. There are two or three posts you may encounter which are useful markers. In the main you will need to keep looking as far ahead as you can and choose the best available sheep-track. With determination it is nearly all rideable, although I do admit to walking intermittently over the last 150 metres to the wood.

Beyond the wood the sheep-tracks will draw you to the only gate. The cairn is now clearly visible – aim for it, and as you arrive you will cross a landrover track. TR with the bigger track which will take you down to the tarmac road, and probably bring you out precisely at a SP. Navigational congratulations will probably be short-lived when you read the inscription. You will find you have ridden down a rutted, 10 metre wide footpath, and you will pass the SP for the actual bridleway (a mere mark in the heather) 200 metres up the road.

## Quarry House to Old Bewick

We quit the tarmac at the first corner after Quarry House at a SP for Blawearie. The line of the bridleway looks reasonably straight on the map, but the reality is somewhat different: so different that posts mark the route, and in a couple of places I am sure you will be pleased to have their confirmation. The first post materialises after 0.89 km, near a rocky outcrop. This is a good place to eat if there is little or no wind. There is time to assess the route ahead and enjoy the wildlife. Alex Spence and I were sitting there one December Sunday having seen snipe, a brace of duck, and trying to identify a little brown bird that was playing hide-and-seek in the heather, when a falcon of some description lifted only metres in front of us as we sat. We were so taken aback that there was no positive identification, but a peregrine got the vote. He must have been having his meal. It is a great spot if the weather is kind. Follow the posts. The track winds its way across the moor towards a huge box cabin above Blawearie. The box is associated with an archaeological site nearby. The track becomes more entertaining the farther you go. There are technical bits with rocks half blocking the tracks, little ditches that tempt you to try and ride them, and a ford that seems very easy but always needs a dab with one foot on the exit. I have promised myself that one day I will ride across it without flying over the handlebars! The ruined Blawearie comes all too soon then it is simply down, down all the way to Old Bewick on a very bumpy farm road. But of course you could always divert across towards Tick Law on one of the other bridleways – if you are confident enough.

*Right: Ingram & Alnham. Autumn at Alnhammoor.*

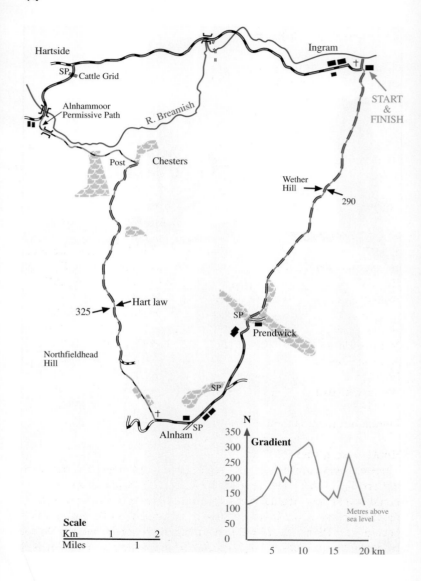

Hartside

SP — Cattle Grid

Alnhammoor
Permissive Path

R. Breamish

Chesters

Post

Ingram

START
&
FINISH

Wether
Hill ← 290

Hart law

325 →

Northfieldhead
Hill

SP

Prendwick

SP

† 

Alnham

SP

**N**

**Gradient**

350
300
250
200
150
100
50
0

Metres above
sea level

5    10    15    20 km

**Scale**

Km        1        2
Miles          1

# 12 Ingram & Alnham

| | |
|---|---|
| **Grade** | 17 Strenuous |
| **19 km** | **(11.8 Miles)** |
| **8.8 km** | Tarmac |
| **7.6 km** | Farm/Estate Road |
| **0.13 km** | Forest Track/Path |
| **2.5 km** | Moorland Track/Path |
| **High Points:** | Hart Law 325m, Wether Hill 290m |
| **Map:** | Ordnance Survey, Landranger 81 Alnwick & Morpeth, Explorer OL16 Cheviot Hills |
| **Facilities:** | Ice Cream at Information Centre in season |

## PLOTTING PLAN

| *START:* | Approach | Map Reference | Depart |
|---|---|---|---|
| Ingram Information Centre | – | 019163 | S |
| Hartside | E | 976162 | SSE |
| Alnhammoor | NNE | 972154 | S |
| Chesters | NW | 986147 | SW |
| HART LAW | NW | 987127 | SSE |
| Northfieldhead Hill | N | 984$^1$/$_2$118$^1$/$_2$ | S |
| Alnham Church | NW | 990109 | E |
| Prendwick | S | 003$^1$/$_2$124$^1$/$_2$ | NE |
| WETHER HILL | SW | 014143 | NE |
| *FINISH:* | | | |
| Ingram Information Centre | S | 019163 | – |

## Route Description

There are not many days of the year when you will not see someone on the first leg of this route, between Ingram and Hartside. It is one of the bonniest and most popular Northumbrian valleys. Usually referred to as the Ingram Valley, the watercourse is actually the River Breamish which becomes the River Till at Chillingham, Ingram being the hamlet. Do not be put off by the relatively high proportion of tarmac we cover. You will find that it not only has a character of its own, but gives access to some great terrain. This is a very open route with a tremendous feeling of space on the watershed at Hart Law. I shrink from saying that it can be bleak at any time of year, but certainly goes up at least two grades if the weather is at all inclement. Once on the hill the only practical way off is either to continue or retrace your route. Ingram is the true home of the Cheviot sheep today. They have an all white fleece and friendly all white faces – right canny beasts. When Beamish Museum set up their farm it was to Ingram that they came for their sheep.

## Ingram to Hartside

Park at the Northumberland National Park Information Centre which is hidden away behind the church. The first phase is all tarmac. Retrace from the Information Centre to the valley road, bear L through Ingram and head W for the hills. Keep R with the road across the purple bridge at the foot of Brough Law after 2.75 km, despite the temptation of what appears to be a good track sneaking off to the L around the base of the hill. It is not – it only goes as far as the wood around the corner. The first bit of tarmac with character hits you as you climb past Greensidehill. How this bit of road does not rate a steep hill marker on the O.S. map amazes me. Or is it the fact that there is often a westerly wind blowing down the hill that makes it ten times harder. No excuses, don't you dare dismount!

## Hartside to Alnham

At Hartside we TL. There is a SP for Alnhammoor and a notice saying Private Road, but it is OK for bikes. We follow the tarmac for 1.2 km to Alnhammoor, turning L just before reaching the farm. Our bridleway is shown going through the farm and around the S side of the river. However, in an effort to prevent folk needlessly passing through the yard, a permissive path has been negotiated which cuts off the corner. There is a discreet, low level SP pointing the way across the grass below the house. Aim for the wicket gate in the corner at the vegetable patch.

Pause and look at the next phase as you close the wicket, because there could be confusion. We need to go through three gates in quick succession, crossing the burn on the way. You cannot see it from the wicket but there is a bridge in among the enclosures. If you are checking the map, it is the lower bridleway we are following, closest to the river. There is also a stile at the last gate and from here you can see our grassy track going straight across the field to the next gate 0.35 km away. In the distance you can see the cutting, up through the trees that will eventually take us over the lip of the valley to Chesters. The field beyond the classic five-bar gate is usually under cultivation, or at least part of it might be. Despite the fact that the map shows the route of the bridleway going straight across, it would be more understanding to veer L to the perimeter fence and follow it to the far corner, only then turning R and aiming for the corner of the wood. It is also more entertaining to ride the edge.

There are two wicket gates at the corner of the wood. Use the one with the stile and the blue bridleway arrow, then up through the trees to the wicket at the far end. On exiting the wood keep straight ahead on this bearing then bear slightly L with the path. It is not a motorway but you will not get lost. You are aiming for the lip of the valley and the path will take you there. Before you know it you will arrive at the gate in the fence. Go through the gate on the obvious path and over the crest by a post keeping the little wood on your L. Chesters is hidden by the copse, and a good moorland road lies between you and the far wood. Another 200 metres will reveal all. TR onto the moorland road at the white-tipped post which pokes out from its little cairn of protective boulders. You can now see a red road winding away up the hill to a gate on the ridge. We follow this road over the moor for 3.21 km. The first gate that we saw from the post arrives over 0.5 km. 400 metres farther on we bear R with the 'main' road keeping another little wood on our L. This is the only junction, so you cannot go wrong. After a further 1.3 km we reach the highest point on the route, Hart Law watershed, 325 m. Incipient burns here feed the Rivers Breamish, Aln and Coquet which ultimately reach the seas as much as 54 km apart – after the Breamish has become the Till, a main tributary of the Tweed..

Exactly 1 km further on our red road turns hairpin L just over the top of Northfield Hill. A large heap of stones marks the corner. This is where we fork slight R to drop down to Alnham. Take care not to lose too much height. If you reach a metal gate you have gone too far. Initially use the sheep-track to aim for the wicket gate in the wall and ride across towards it. After 50 or 60 metres look down to the wall and you will see our gate in the corner. We follow the wall down to the trees above Alnharn using the obvious bridleway. It is a bit of a test at the first of the trees due to prevailing wet conditions. Continue down this track all the way to Alnham, starting the final drop to the church quite slowly because you inevitably speed up quite a lot in the middle section! On reaching the tarmac road, TL towards Alnham. There is a nice wide verge and a stout wall – a convenient place to have your bait, the best protection so far.

## Alnham to Ingram

TL again at Alnham following the SP to Prendwick (pronounced Prendick) some 1.6 km distant. This large farm provides a series of right-angle turns. We follow the road R at the buildings and L down the side of the cattle pens. When the road goes tightly R at the cottages, we go straight on through a gateway onto the loose again. A small SP indicates INGRAM 3. Occasionally the gate is closed. This last leg provides a great bit of off-road with which to finish – testing farm road which gives way to ancient compacted grass, then the final field down to Ingram. Immediately beyond the gateway the loose road veers R through a shallow ford and along to a gate, which is normally closed. The track can be quite muddy at the gate, but it soon dries as it turns L and climbs steadily. About 0.6 km beyond the closed gate our track goes SO onto grass to the nearest gate in the fence which runs right down the hillside. Do not be tempted by the stony red road climbing to the higher gate. The beautiful, compacted grass track now takes you to the top of Wether Hill, 275m, with a couple of minor impediments in the way of squelchy bits – which are rideable with a degree of determination. Pause at the top and enjoy the view because it is down all the way now, 2.1 km. Two gates punctuate the descent, but perhaps it is just as well, because the latter part becomes quite uneven and high-speed rut swapping invariably leads to disaster.

Nick Eley took such a shaking on one descent that one of his contact lenses became dislodged. There followed an incredible display of out-of-focus leg flailing and rut swapping which culminated in an unceremonious dumping of a tired and muddy mountain biker in the ditch. Be warned! All too soon the double gates at Ingram are reached and it is all over except the toddle along to the carpark and a well-deserved ice cream if the Centre is open. Now you know your way, you can do it the other way round. It is just as good.

***Deel's Hill.*** *We bet you've always wondered where the keeper of maps at the Bodleian, Oxford spends his days off. Now you know, Deel's Hill!*

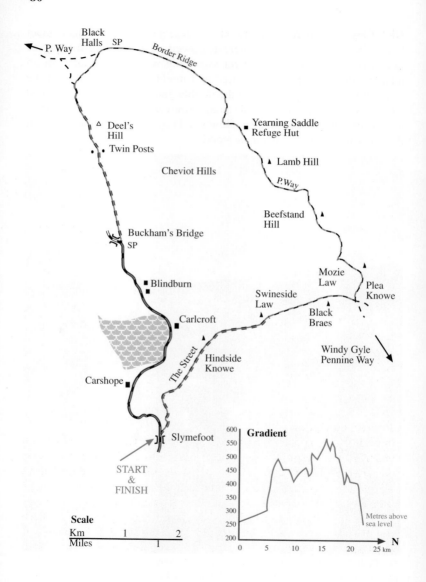

# 13 Deel's Hill & The Border Ridge

| | |
|---|---|
| **Grade** | 21 Expert – a real test. |
| **22.21 km** | **(13.8 Miles)** |
| **17.44 km** | Moorland Track/Path |
| **4.77 km** | Tarmac |
| **High Points:** | Deel's Hill 495m, Lamb Hill 511m, Beefstand Hill 562m, Mozie Law 552m |
| **Maps:** | Ordnance Survey, Landranger 80 Cheviot Hills & Kielder Water, Explorer OL16 Cheviot Hills. |
| **Facilities:** | None. Mountain Refuge Hut at 804129 |

## PLOTTING PLAN

| *START:* | Approach | Map Reference | Depart |
|---|---|---|---|
| Slymefoot (Rowhope Rd End) | – | 80/860114$^1$/$_2$ | W |
| Buckham's Bridge | ENE | 824107 | W |
| Deel's Hill | ENE | 804101$^1$/$_2$ | WSW |
| Border Ridge (Black Halls) | SSW | 789106 | N |
| Yearning Saddle Hut | SW | 804129 | NE |
| Lamb Hill | SW | 810$^1$/$_2$133 | NE |
| Beefstand Hill | WSW | 821144 | NE |
| Plea Knowe | WNW | 835150 | SSW |
| Hindside Knowe | WNW | 846120 | ESE |
| *FINISH:* | | | |
| Slymefoot | W | 860114$^1$/$_2$ | – |

## Route Description

In both winter and summer this is a dry route. Even when conditions underfoot are verging on saturation, there is no drinkable water – so go prepared. The first time I traversed this section of the Border Ridge, I injured my arm dragging the bike repeatedly from seemingly bottomless peat hags. Since that time a rash of excellent duckboards have appeared, some now so well-established that they are nearly overgrown with rushes. But they are a tremendous improvement and make the Ridge the exhilarating experience it should be when conditions are good. On the other hand, this route can be a very serious undertaking in bad weather. The route is still quite elevated in the latter stages as was graphically demonstrated between Swineside Law and Hindside Knowe one January day. Malcolm Williams, who was always fitter than me, failed to catch me up after tending the gate and allowing me to ride on. Eventually, I stopped to see where he was. When he arrived he said, "I've had a blow out." "A puncture?" "No. The back wheel just blown out from beneath me on the last col." On a nice day you will wonder what all the fuss was about. On a bad day – run for the valley. Be warned.

### Slymefoot to The Border Ridge

You will not find Slymefoot at Rowhope Road End marked on maps anymore – but where the Rowhope Burn enters the Coquet there is a large rock on the north bank, the base of the bridge abutment now. Close to this rock, in the eighteenth century, stood the Slymefoot public house, a den of iniquity and the winter quarters of all the neighbouring sheep farmers who reputedly spent all their time gambling and drinking while their shepherds came in every day to receive their orders and carry the news. The whisky at the Slymefoot was the product of the illicit distilleries, then quite common among the hills of the Upper Coquet – real 'mountain dew'.

There is parking at the White Bridge at Slymefoot. The only tarmac on the route comes first – ideal to get the legs working fully before the first ascent. Set off W up Upper Coquetdale past Carshope, Carlcroft and Blindburn, turning off onto the green road just before Buckham's Bridge. There is a SP pointing up the obvious track to Deel's Hill, which is rideable in dry conditions. The gate at the top is often open, but it is a good place to pause and have a look around. Beyond the gate are two small direction poles. Keep L for Deel's Hill, then having reached the summit zoom down and head for the Border Ridge. The official version of our route turns R onto a rabbit track to remain faithful to the bridleway, but if you miss it do not worry. You will meet the Border Fence a bit further S than intended, but still TR and head for Lamb Hill on the Pennine Way.

## The Border Ridge

*Examination of the map will show you that you can extend this route in either direction along the Border Ridge. Try it sometime.*

TR on a well-defined track and shoot down to Black Halls where a SP points the way to Lamb Hill. From now on you will encounter several lichen-encrusted SPs which say nothing but you will know what they mean in any case. Three km onwards you will reach the Yearning Saddle Mountain Refuge: a welcome shelter on many days, and an excellent place to have your bait. Then climb up to the summit of Lamb Hill, descend a bit and cycle over a tremendous stretch of duckboarding. Next you climb to Beefstand Hill which, at 561m, is the highest point of the day. The Border Fence is a wonderful navigational aid. Even when engulfed in cloud simply stick dose to it and mark off the corners on your map to keep you right. The last summit to climb is Mozie Law. Then XRTR at Plea Knowe, which is only marked on the Explorer maps, and head S down The Street towards the 'Danger' board on Black Braes. Plea Knowe junction is the obvious place from which to extend the route. You will be familiar with the going of the day, your pace, and the available time remaining. If everything is in your favour you can climb up to Windy Gyle then descend on an ever-improving track to Trows and finish back at Slymefoot as planned.

## Plea Knowe to Slymefoot

Follow The Street all the way. It is well-defined and one of the best finishes to any route in the Cheviots. The descent from Black Braes to the col beneath Swineside Law is always exciting. Littered with granite marbles when dry, grass like ice when it is wet, and if it is icy – hold onto your hat! Between Swineside Law and Hindside Knowe, pick the best current line then tighten your straps for the final plummet at the galvanised gate. Again follow the best line down the grassy track. It gets better and better, faster and faster, culminating in a slither down to Slymefoot that will test all your skills and equipment. What is your verdict? Is this not the best finish in the county?

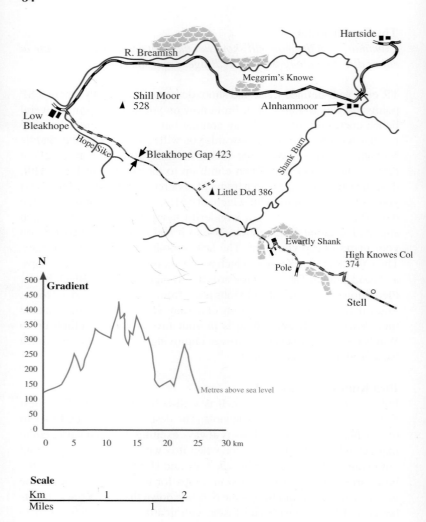

Hartside

R. Breamish

Meggrim's Knowe

Shill Moor
▲ 528

Low
Bleakhope

Alnhammoor →

Hope Sike

↓ Bleakhope Gap 423

Shank Burn

▲ Little Dod 386

Ewartly Shank

High Knowes Col
374

Pole

Stell

**N**

**Gradient**

| 500 |
| 450 |
| 400 |
| 350 |
| 300 |
| 250 |
| 200 |
| 150 |
| 100 |
| 50 |
| 0 |

Metres above sea level

0    5    10    15    20    25    30 km

**Scale**

| Km | | 1 | | 2 |
| Miles | | | 1 | |

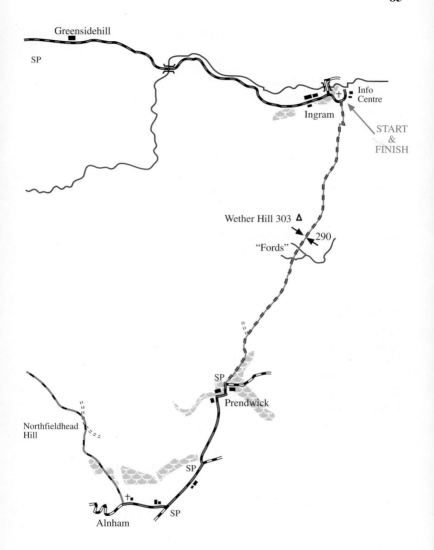

Greensidehill

SP

Info
Centre

Ingram

START
&
FINISH

Wether Hill 303 ∆
290

"Fords"

SP

Prendwick

Northfieldhead
Hill

SP

SP

Alnham

# 14 Ingram, Bleakhope & Alnham

| | |
|---|---|
| **Grade** | 20 Strenuous |
| **25.4 km** | **(15.8 Miles)** |
| **7.65 km** | Moorland Track/Path |
| **0.34 km** | Forest Track/Path |
| **3.72 km** | Farm/Estate Road |
| **13.66 km** | Tarmac |
| **High Points:** | Bleakhope Gap 423m, Little Dod 386m, High Knowes Col 374m, Wether Hill 290m |
| **Maps:** | Ordnance Survey, Landrangers 81 Alnwick & Morpeth, 80 Cheviot Hills & Kielder Water,  Explorer OL16 Cheviot Hills |
| **Facilities:** | Light refreshments at Information Centre in season. Usually Easter to October. |

## PLOTTING PLAN

| *START:* | Approach | Map Reference | Depart |
|---|---|---|---|
| National Park Info. Centre | – | 81/020163$^{1}/_{2}$ | S |
| Hartside | E | 976162 | SSE |
| Meggrim's Knowe | E | 962155 | W |
| Low Bleakhope | NE | 80/934$^{1}/_{2}$153 | SE |
| Bleakhope Gap | NW | 943$^{1}/_{2}$146$^{1}/_{2}$ | SE |
| Little Dod | NW | 81/952141 | SE |
| Snow Pole | NW | 964133 | ENE |
| High Knowes Col | NW | 970$^{1}/_{2}$130$^{1}/_{2}$ | SE |
| Northfieldhead Hill Corner | N | 984$^{1}/_{2}$118$^{1}/_{2}$ | S |
| Alnham | NW | 990109 | E |
| Prendwick Cottages | S | 003$^{1}/_{2}$124$^{1}/_{2}$ | NE |
| Wether Hill | SW | 013143 | NE |
| *FINISH:* | | | |
| National Park Info. Centre | S | 020163$^{1}/_{2}$ | – |

## Route Description

This route was designed as an extension to the Ingram & Alnham loop but turned out to be quite different. Apart from being longer, it is a much more serious proposition. Not only does it reach greater height, the route itself is more difficult to follow and in places is quite strength-sapping. It might seem odd to say that one of the major climbs is on tarmac, but the push beyond Meggrim's Knowe towards Shill Moor always kills me for some reason. See what you think. The other two climbs are just about rideable if you are fortunate with the conditions. Excessive wet will make the Salters Road from Low Bleakhope unrideable near the head of Hope Sike, and the so called fords on Wether Hill will need a lot of strength and determination late in the day to avoid a few metres walk. Having said all that, the route has become one of my favourite loops: old commercial roads in a great situation, and the descent from Little Dod to Shank Burn thrown in. This one you will enjoy, I promise.

## Ingram to Low Bleakhope

There is limited parking at the Information Centre, but ample space at the toilets near the bridge. The route starts at the Information Centre and travels W up the valley from Ingram, but can just as easily commence from wherever you park. Take care as you ride through the farm.

This section is entirely tarmac but good stuff nonetheless. If you have never been up the Breamish valley (more usually called the Ingram Valley) before, take your time and admire the countryside. Note the steepness of the hills. About 1 km W of Ingram Farm have a good look at the screes on the far side of the river, and the lack of vegetation on them. It is like a stony, mini-desert in a fertile valley. You may also see what I believe to be a Northumbrian phenomenon – purple and white foxgloves growing together. I have seen them in several places on the S and E side of the Cheviots, but they are pretty reliable down by the river at Ingram. The bank at Greensidehill is the first test. Don't you dare get off, it's only tarmac! Then TL onto the 'Private Road' and along to Alnhammoor. Stay on the tarmac to the climb beyond Meggrim's Knowe mentioned earlier. The road drops steeply along the N side of Shill Moor and in winter never gets the warm sun. Watch out for ice. On reaching Low Bleakhope TL onto the gravel track down to the ford behind the bungalow and prepare for the next climb.

## Low Bleakhope to Alnham

One late December day, three of us did this loop and nearly succeeded in riding all the way from Low Bleakhope to Bleakhope Gap mainly because the ground was frozen. I failed with cramp; Graeme and John capitulated with the giggles ... but I will get them back. The track, the Salters Road, is very good to begin with. It becomes boggy on the flat before the final climb, then improves beyond the gate so you can invariably ride to the summit. There is a speedy descent to the little col prior to Little Dod, then the incomparable plummet to the Shank Burn. There is no standard 'best route' across what is marked on the map as a ford at the burn, because it changes every time there is a hint of a spate. Do what you think is best! Climb steeply away from Shank Burn. Keep R at the top of the hill then through the wood to the farm. Follow the official blue arrows through Ewartly Shank, out on the tarmac through the gates. TL off the road onto an ancient green track at the first real R-hand bend opposite a single snow pole 200 metres after the last gate. Check the map – it will definitely help here. The next 3 km demand a good deal of common sense, concentration and a high degree of moor craft. We follow the Salters Road shown heading SE in a relatively straight line on the map, but modern usage by the shepherd's bike and other rural vehicles tend to lure you off in a couple of places. If you have chosen to use the 1:25,000 Explorer map, you should have no trouble. However, the proper track is so difficult to see that I thought it easier, and safer, to overshoot to the stones and retrace 100 metres, in an effort to ensure that we at least start the least-defined stretch at the right place – the gate. In slight contradiction to the map, the modern path passes quite close to the stell (sheepfold). Stay with it and follow the motor-cycle tracks across an interesting bit of moor to the only gate in the fence. If in doubt, look for the gate. Beyond the gate, the line of the Salters Road continues across the moor to Northfieldhead Hill. It is the only obvious route. Look well ahead and it will seem better defined.

We rejoin the Ingram & Alnham route on Northfieldhead Hill, then follow it exactly. If you need more descriptive directions, please read that route (number 12). 70 metres after joining the compacted red road we leave it. Bear R across the moor again towards a wicket, then a gate in the corner which leads us down between the wall and the hedge to Alnham Church, via a very boggy bit near the trees. If you have not had your bait, Alnham is a good place to take it. There is shelter against the church wall, a little pond that always provides some wildfowl amusement, and it is usually 5 degrees C warmer than in the surrounding hills. TL when you reach the tarmac by the church, then L again at the junction and follow the signs to Prendwick.

## Alnham to Ingram

The tarmac from Alnham to Prendwick can be either a good way to get going again after lunch, or a respite before the final off-road stretch over the top to Ingram. Prendwick is such a large farm that the road is forced to follow its shape. So it is TJTR, then 90L. When it turns 90R again at the cottages, we go SO through a gate onto a loose farm road towards Ingram. There is a SP to confirm the route. In theory we follow this track all the way to Ingram. In practice there is only one place where you might make a mistake. Stick with the obvious road, but after 0.88 km the compacted track veers L higher up the hillside than we need to go. At this point we go SO across the grass to a gate which is only 70 metres away, and then the road is obvious again. By now you will have attuned to the fact that we will be riding grass from here to the top. This is a beautiful bit of grass, always short and only just poking through the very firm base – a great old road. Near the summit there are a couple of squelchy bits which used to be fords in the days when this was a commercial route. I suppose they still are, but have attracted a lot of reeds. The attendant silt demands a fair amount of effort and technique to make a successful crossing. Good luck. I always stop on the col of

Wether Hill and have a look around. It is low enough not to be too bleak, but high enough to afford extensive views of the Cheviot fringes. I really like it. I hope you do too. And then it is down all the way to Ingram. Please do not get carried away in the ruts, many of us have. Paul Eynon, a mountain bike racer of some stature at the time, left his bike completely near the bottom and took the seat out of his shorts, also near the bottom – be warned. Despite the shaking, we reach the double gates at Ingram all too soon, and that is it.

*Bleakhope. Nancies! What's wrong with riding it?*

**Middle Route.** *Looking NW from the top of Pass Peth, the final climb of Middle Route to Shilmoor, Upper Coquetdale. Part of the bridelway we use between the two can be seen running L to R across the lower fellside.*

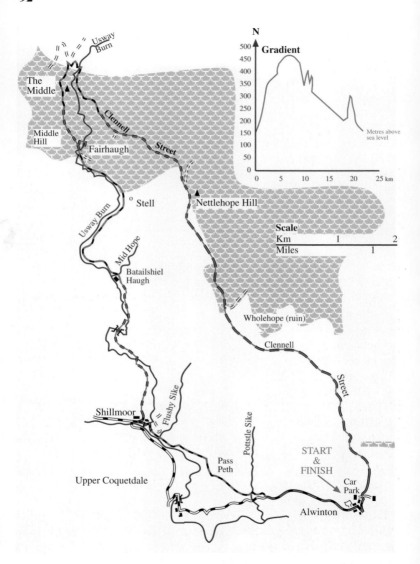

# 15 Middle Route

| | |
|---|---|
| **Grade** | 20 Strenuous |
| **21.67 km** | **(13.47 Miles)** |
| **10.65 km** | Moorland Track/Path |
| **3.74 km** | Forest Track/Path |
| **3.16 km** | Farm/Estate Road |
| **2.29 km** | Forest Road |
| **1.83 km** | Tarmac |
| **High Points:** | Nettlehope Hill 470m, The Middle 399m, Pass Peth 299m |
| **Maps:** | Ordnance Survey, Landranger 80 Cheviot Hills & Kielder Water, Explorer OL16 Cheviot Hills |
| **Facilities:** | Public Conveniences at Start. Rose & Thistle just across the road from Finish |

## PLOTTING PLAN

| *START:* | Approach | Map Reference | Depart |
|---|---|---|---|
| Alwinton Carpark | – | 80/920063 | E |
| Clennell Street | S | 922$^{1}$/$_{2}$069 | N |
| Wholehope | SE | 901093 | NW |
| Nettlehope Hill | S | 894115 | NNW |
| Usway Burn | S | 876136 | N |
| The Middle | N | 874134 | S |
| Fairhaugh | NNE | 876122 | SSE |
| Batailshiel Haugh | NW | 882102 | SE |
| Shillmoor | NNW | 886077 | SE |
| Pass Peth | NW | 897$^{1}$/$_{2}$068$^{1}$/$_{2}$ | SE |
| *FINISH:* | | | |
| Alwinton Carpark | W | 920063 | – |

## Route Description

This is called the Middle Route because it is about halfway up the scale of difficulty in the guide; (or at least until the advent of Tim King's grading system!) it actually crosses a hill called The Middle, and even if it is not geographically exact you certainly feel as if you are in the middle of The Cheviots. I am ashamed to say that there was one section of this route I had never ridden before covering it for the book, and it is excellent. This was the ancient route over the Pass Peth from Shillmoor to Alwinton, the last leg of the tour. David Dippie Dixon in his wonderful book 'Upper Coquetdale' provides the best description. 'Far above on the left bank of the river rise lofty cliffs of a great height. The face of this acclivity is traversed by 'Passpeth', a perilous path, nothing more than a sheep-track overlooking the linns, to be trod only by those possessed of a sure foot and a clear head.' It is now a lot wider than this description. I suspect that it grew in magnitude due to the passage of 'traffic' and only fell into disuse after the new bridge was built at Linbriggs in 1936. Today it is but a small splendid stretch of an extremely varied route.

## Alwinton to The Middle

This section is exactly the same as the start of Clennell Street & Salters Road, and is well worth doing before you attempt the longer loop. TL out of the Alwinton carpark, past the Rose and Thistle, then out of the village following the SP for the Border Ridge. This is Clennell Street; steep and stony to begin with, then soft and squelchy when the gradient eases. Up to and beyond Wholehope it gets wetter but solid, before joining the Forestry road that takes you over Nettlehope Hill. There is a grassy 100 metre stretch when we bear L to remain faithful to Clennell Street. Then a lumpier forest road takes us all the way to the edge of the forest and the start of the exciting sheep-track descent to the Usway Burn. Halfway down this descent there is a large patch of rushes. Keep as high as you can. It is not necessarily drier, but it is much firmer and you will not grind to a halt in the stinking bog. Take care also at the wooden bridge if it is wet or even damp. The sheep persistently impregnate it producing a surface akin to ice even when there is merely a hint of dampness in the air.

Beyond the bridge follow the bridleway arrows through the gate, up the hill, then over the fence. The stile marks the junction of three bridleways.

We TL, back past the hut, through the gate (or over the stile) and straight up The Middle. The true line of the bridleway contours around the hill, but the track used by the shepherd takes a direct line over the top. There seems no point in creating a new mark on the hillside so stick with the ruts and see if you can make the summit without recourse to walking.

## The Middle to Shillmoor
Following the valley of the Usway Burn, you are bound to see birdlife. This is the ornithological section. The October day on which I checked this route was one of the best. As soon as I crested The Middle an old heron lifted off the burn far below, flapped downstream a couple of hundred metres, then settled again screened by the pines. The next encounter came less than a kilometre farther on as I climbed Middle Hill. I could hear honking, and sure enough as I reached the crest before descending the muddy hill, there were geese tucking into some tasty vegetation. I think I slipped by without being seen because the honking continued and I never saw them lift off. South of Fairhaugh, a goldcrest ushered me through the wood. It is always great to see Britain's smallest bird. Then beyond the stell I rounded a corner to surprise four herons. They looked like young birds but I have never seen so many out in the open. Underneath one of the bridges beyond Batailshiel Haugh a trio of wigeon lifted ahead of me and then as I crossed the structure the last one shot out, just to give me a gliff. You always see dippers on the Upper Coquet and I was not disappointed. The sight of a ring ouzel pleased me, but I could not help thinking that it could have been a blackbird partly because it was flying away from me (as they always seem to do) and also because it was about time he should have been heading south to overwinter in North Africa. My final treat was half a dozen huge crows behaving in a very strange manner on a hilltop beyond the Pass Peth. I surmised that a dead sheep was the cause of the uproar, but did not fancy the extra climb to confirm my theory. In any case stopping to watch them was a good excuse, when really I was recovering from the climb.

## Back to the route.
Follow the tractor track down off The Middle, through the gate with the

deep pool at the bottom. Then climb straight up over the side of Middle Hill and down towards Fairhaugh. There is a great ford at Fairhaugh, only just rideable, and even then only when the bedrocks are arranged favourably – consequently it is a summer test. My success rate is about one in five! The sensible winter alternative is the bridge gained by turning sharp L at the corner near the bottom of the hill. This too can be a bit hazardous when wet, so take care because it is a fair drop into the water. Beyond Fairhaugh our bridleway shrinks considerably. It follows the eastern bank of Usway Burn. You have to look hard to find the tiny path which leaves the road only 20 metres up from the old farmhouse to start this section. Initially, the path hugs the barbed wire-topped fence so be prepared to walk if it is slippery underfoot. The situation soon improves and the weave through the trees is great. Many branches cross the track forming a tunnel and you will be glad of your helmet and glasses. If you manage to ride all the way to the stile at the stell without at least one reassuring dab, you'll have done well.

A stell is a round sheepfold. This one is a fine example and provides excellent protection on a windy day – a good lunch halt. The track beyond the stell is usually just rideable and improves as you near Batailshiel Haugh. Follow the arrows around the farm, encountering en route the dinky ford through the Mid Hope. Aim for the 'main' road and follow it all the way to Shillmoor.

## Shillmoor to Alwinton

At Shillmoor go around the front of the farm buildings, across the farm bridge then stick close to the wall. The bridleway hugs the wall despite the obvious temptation to climb the hill on a good road. Use the stile beneath the hairpin bend to get down to the Flushey Sike. Then simply follow the ancient route gently up and around the fellside. You can see the green track stretching out before you. All you need to do is follow your nose and the bridleway arrows to the Pass Peth. This is the obvious track climbing D.D. Dixon's 'acclivity' – you cannot miss it. Pause at the top of Pass Peth and imagine spending all day and many nights here guarding against the incursions of the Scottish freebooters. But do not get me wrong – many of the residents of Coquetdale were not averse to doing a little shifting for their living. On the summit look for the little posts with the arrows, then stiles and gates guide you down the last part of the bridleway. Eventually you come to a hunting gate beyond the rocky-bottomed Pottstle Sike where we join the tarmac for the final flee to Alwinton. Every really good mountain bike route should finish with a good downhill. This one happens to be on tarmac, but if you do not touch 50 kph then you are not trying.

***The Street.*** *Confession time. I have **never** managed to ride all the way up here. As you can see, some have. The obvious thing to do is ride it anticlockwise, the way it is described in the book and ride **down** this bit of The Street*

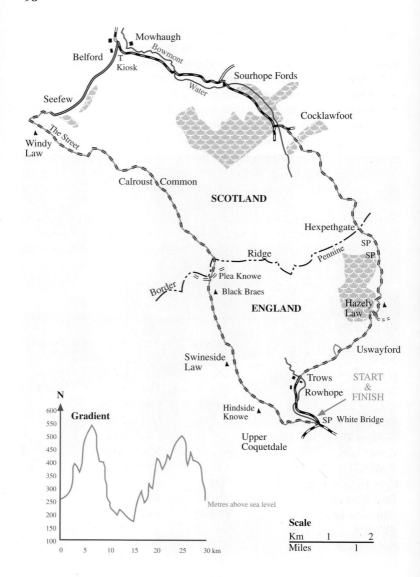

Mowhaugh

Belford

T Kiosk

Bowmont

Sourhope Fords

Seefew

Water

Cocklawfoot

The Street

▲ Windy Law

Calroust Common

**SCOTLAND**

Hexpethgate

SP

Ridge

Pennine

SP

Border

Plea Knowe

▲ Black Braes

**ENGLAND**

Hazely Law ▲

Swineside Law ▲

Uswayford

Trows

START & FINISH

Rowhope

Hindside Knowe ▲

SP White Bridge

Upper Coquetdale

**N**

**Gradient**

600
550
500
450
400
350
300
250
200
150
100

Metres above sea level

0    5    10    15    20    25    30 km

**Scale**

Km    1    2
Miles    1

## 16 The Street

| | |
|---|---|
| **Grade** | 21 Expert |
| **29.62 km** | **(18.4 Miles)** |
| **18.29 km** | Moorland Track/Path |
| **5.ll km** | Farm/Estate Road |
| **6.22 km** | Tarmac |
| **High Points:** | Hexpethgate 537m, Plea Knowe 509m |
| **Maps:** | Ordnance Survey, Landrangers 80 Cheviot Hills & Kielder Water and 74 Kelso & Coldstream. The vast majority of the route is on Landranger 80 or Explorer OL16 Cheviot Hills |
| **Facilities:** | None. This is a fairly remote and exposed route. Be well prepared. It is essential that you take a map in case of retreat or escape from the high ground. |

## PLOTTING PLAN

| *START:* | Approach | Map Reference | Depart |
|---|---|---|---|
| Rowhope Road End | – | 80/860114$^{1}/_{2}$ | N |
| Hazely Law Corner | NNW | 874$^{1}/_{2}$138 | N |
| Hexpethgate | SE | 871$^{1}/_{2}$160$^{1}/_{2}$ | NNW |
| Cocklawfoot | SE | 853$^{1}/_{2}$185$^{1}/_{2}$ | W |
| Sourhope Road End | E | 839197$^{1}/_{2}$ | W |
| Belford Telephone Kiosk | SE | 74/815208 | SW |
| Ruin Corner | NE | 80/799191$^{1}/_{2}$ | NW |
| THE STREET | NE | 792190$^{1}/_{2}$ | SE |
| Spot Height 430m | NW | 823173$^{1}/_{2}$ | SE |
| Plea Knowe | NNE | 835150 | SSW |
| Hindside Knowe | WNW | 847120 | ESE |
| *FINISH:* | | | |
| Rowhope Road End | W | 860114$^{1}/_{2}$ | – |

## Route Description

Navigationally this is an easy route because you can see where the tracks go for most of the tour. If you are very fit, it is all rideable too, being founded on old commercial routes. But for normal folk it is a good test, and if the weather turns against you it can be horrendous. One February day when the forecast was good we set off, in a company of about fifteen Snipes and Moonters, from Belford on Bowmont. By the time we reached Calroust Common an innocuous little cloud had decided to hit us with a very local blizzard which persisted all the way to the Border Ridge. But by the time we had descended to Upper Coquetdale and dined, the sun was out again and we re-crossed the Ridge in glorious sunshine. For this one make sure you get the weather forecast and watch the clouds as you ride the loop.

## Rowhope Road End to Belford

There is parking space at the White Bridge (which has recently been painted light blue!) at Rowhope Road End and a SP pointing the way to Rowhope and Uswayford. The tarmac only goes as far as Trows. At Trows, follow the main red road over Murder Cleugh col and on to Hazely Law corner. Then turn hairpin L onto a green road which will take you all the way over the Border Ridge to Cocklawfoot. Look ahead as you drop down from the col and you will see the track climbing up the W side of Hazely Law. This will give you a good idea of where it joins the main road, because there is no SP and it is not the easiest slot to hit if you do not have a computer. Once on this northern spur of Clennell Street, all you have to do is follow it ever upwards to the Border Ridge at Hexpethgate. There are a couple of bridleways branching off on the R in the upper stages – but if in doubt go up!

The Pennine Way is crossed as you enter Scotland with a tremendous panorama of the Cheviot Hills and the Scottish Borders beyond. Then go down to Cocklawfoot still on a green road which will let you go as fast as you dare, sheep permitting. TL at Cocklawfoot and follow the tarmac downstream all the way to Belford taking care at the Sourhope fords. They can be green and slippery in summer, icy in winter, but always great fun due to the high speed approach. I assume the alternative bridges are OK but I have never known anyone use them. Mountain bikers must be mad. In winter especially you will probably see quite a few duck on the Bowmont Water and perhaps even domestic geese near Mowhaugh Farm. Then look out for the telephone kiosk at Belford where we TL for the second phase.

## Belford to The Street

There is a SP next to the kiosk but nothing on it for us. We simply head SW along past the cottage and follow our noses. The track becomes greener the farther we follow it. Then, after passing the ruin of the aptly named Seefew, there is the amazing grassy climb to the wall of the N side of Windy Law that marks our connection with The Street itself.

## The Street

Do not go through the gate in the wall. TL and stick close to the NE side of the wall following it SE. You will soon get the feeling of the track. Jink R and L at the next slipgate and after that you cannot go wrong. There are some great sections: classic rutted 3-ply where riding upon the heather in the middle is the easiest option; pure moorland that is fast and bumpy; little technical bits caused by natural erosion. After you cross the Border Ridge back into England at Plea Knowe, you get a terrific descent into Upper Coquetdale. Even the Moonters agree that it is crazy. Beautiful, green, compacted track punctuated by soft peaty holes. If you are going fast enough you will probably jump them. If not you will be flying without the bike at 30 mph. Evasive action can produce excessive excitement as can the very last steep bit. All too soon you are back at the White Bridge, and hopefully still in one piece!

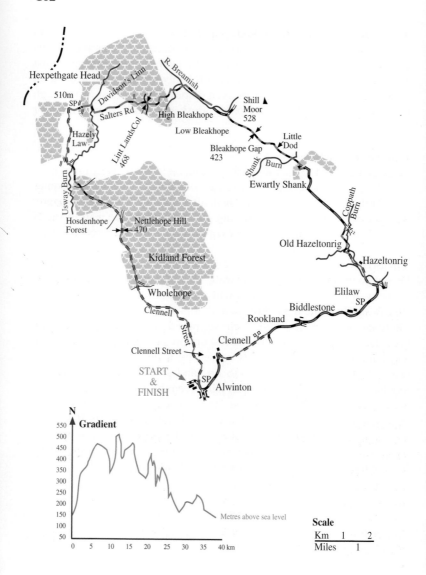

Hexpethgate Head

510m
SP

Davidson's Linn

R. Breamish

Shill
Moor
528

Salters Rd

High Bleakhope

Hazely
Law

Low Bleakhope

Little
Dod

Lint LandsCol
468

Bleakhope Gap
423

Shank    Burn

Usway Burn

Ewartly Shank

Hosdenhope
Forest

Nettlehope Hill
470

Coppath Burn

Kidland Forest

Old Hazeltonrig

Hazeltonrig

Wholehope

Elilaw
SP

Biddlestone

Clennell

Street

Rookland

Clennell Street

Clennell

START
&
FINISH

SP   Alwinton

**N**

**Gradient**

550
500
450
400
350
300
250
200
150
100
50

Metres above sea level

0    5    10    15    20    25    30    35    40 km

**Scale**

Km    1         2

Miles    1

# 17   Clennell Street & Salters Road

| | |
|---|---|
| **Grade** | 21 Expert |
| **37.7 km** | **(23.4 Miles)** |
| **9.05 km** | Moorland Track/Path |
| **3.78 km** | Forest Track/Path |
| **10.8 km** | Farm/Estate Road |
| **4.31 km** | Forest Road |
| **9.81 km** | Tarmac |
| **High Points:** | Nettlehope Hill 470m, Hexpethgate Approach 510m, Lint Lands Col 468m, Bleakhope Gap 423m, Little Dod 386m |
| **Maps:** | Ordnance Survey, Landrangers 80 Cheviot Hills & Kielder Water, 81 Alnwick & Morpeth , Explorer OL16 Cheviot Hills |
| **Facilities:** | Pub, Grub & Camping, Rose & Thistle, Alwinton; Clennell Hall, Alwinton. Chalets & Caravan Site Clennell Hall. |

## PLOTTING PLAN

| START: | Approach | Map Reference | Depart |
|---|---|---|---|
| Alwinton Carpark | – | 80/920063 | E |
| Clennell Street | S | 922$^{1}/_{2}$069 | N |
| Wholehope | SE | 901093 | NW |
| Nettlehope Hill | S | 894115 | NNW |
| Usway Burn | S | 876136 | N |
| Hazely Law | SSW | 875144 | N |
| Hexpethgate Approach | SSE | 875157 | SE |
| Davidson's Linn | SW | 884157 | SE |
| Lint Lands Col | W | 904158 | E |
| Low Bleakhope | NW | 934$^{1}/_{2}$153 | SE |
| Bleakhope Gap | NW | 943147 | SE |
| Little Dod | NW | 81/952$^{1}/_{2}$141 | ESE |
| Coppath Burn | NW | 976$^{1}/_{2}$114$^{1}/_{2}$ | SSW |
| Hazeltonrig | NW | 981101 | ESE |

|  | **Approach** | **Map Reference** | **Depart** |
|---|---|---|---|
| Scrainwood | WNW | 988094$^{1}/_{2}$ | S |
| Elilaw | ESE | 975085$^{1}/_{2}$ | W |
| Biddlestone | E | 955081$^{1}/_{2}$ | WSW |
| Rookland | ENE | 80/943077 | WSW |
| Clennell Road End | ENE | 922061 | NNW |
| *FINISH:* |  |  |  |
| Alwinton Carpark | E | 920063 | – |

## Route Description

This is a serious route for real mountain bikers. If you are good enough it is rideable all the way round, with the possible exception of the first hundred metres away from Davidson's Linn which never seems to be dry enough to get sufficient grip, even if you are very fit and have the necessary technique. There are three major climbs: Clennell Street itself; the ascent of the W side of Hazely Law to Hexpethgate Approach; and the Shill Moor track to Bleakhope Gap, which starts well-compacted and finishes on grass. There is also the little savage stint from the Shank Burn to the wood at the top of the hill which is rideable only if conditions are perfect; and coming as it does late in the day, it is always an easy decision to walk. And of course there are downhills to match. The off-camber descent to the Usway Burn is always good entertainment. Then when you TR off the N end of Clennell Street onto the Salters Road near Hexpethgate, the track through the forest down to Davidson's Linn has a character all of its own, with the final 50 metres down to the waterfall a real test of skill and nerve. The ride down to the infant River Breamish from Lint Lands demands all your moorland trailcraft just to stay on the bike, and you have to find your way too. But the *pièce de reésistance* is the hurtle down from Little Dod to the Shank Burn. It is something else. But beware – there is a fence at the very bottom. You are supposed to ride across the ford, not fly into it.

Combined with these main elements there is just about every type of off-road going you can imagine; from well-compacted ancient roads, through squelchy forest cuttings, to stretches of sphagnum which are very difficult to assess and very easy to sink into. I reckon all the fords are rideable. Many of my friends, or perhaps ex friends, might disagree. And I admit to using the bridge at the Breamish if it is cold or there is anything more than a trickle of water. There are at least four notable fords and an equal number of easier ones. If nothing else, your fording ability is bound to have improved by the time you return to Alwinton.

## Alwinton to Hexpethgate Approach

All you have to do navigationally is follow Clennell Street for 12.13 km from Alwinton to the junction with the Salters Road. TL out of the carpark, past the Rose and Thistle, and onto the track that leads N out of the village. I am sure that no one will mind if you sneak across the little bridge to the SP for Clennell Street. The first part of Clennell Street is stony with bedrock in places, but it is softer on the top as you approach Wholehope. Many years ago there used to be a little Youth Hostel at Wholehope, but now there is only a white shed for the cattle, and a gate with a pool. Follow the wet track into the forest. Soon after you join the forestry road the gradient eases. Cross over to Nettlehope Hill where Clennell Street forks L. Watch for the junction, it is possible to miss it. Go down to the gate into Hosdenhope Forest and NW to Usway Burn. At the edge of the forest there is a knackered gate that always persuades me to use the stile. Then you are into the first descent of note. When you reach the reedy patch keep as high as you can – otherwise you might sink to a stop. Take care at the bridge if it is wet – the sheep have impregnated the wood which makes it like ice when damp. Follow the bridleway arrows up the hill, across the road at the corner and onto the green track up the side of Hazely Law. A serious test awaits at the bends at Hazely Slack, where loose stones add to the difficulty of the gradient. If you ride this, you are good.

Eventually you will be able to see a SP pointing the way to the R. But we want the second one. Both 'junctions' are the same shape which further complicates the issue, but wait until you reach the fingerpost saying

'Salters Road' before you turn R. This junction is the highest point on the route, 510m. From here you can see much of the loop winding its way through the hills, particularly the track of the Salters Road as it cuts its way through the forestry. If you feel inclined you can ride up to the Hexpethgate Head on the Border Ridge only 0.42 km up the track and enjoy the view into Scotland, or is that asking a bit much.

## Hexpethgate Approach to Shank Burn

New SPs point the way to Salters Road through the forest. You cannot go wrong, all you have to do is ride it! Take care crossing the burn at Davidson's Linn. The last SP in the forest is a trifle misleading. It is placed against the road near the edge of the trees pointing E with the main thoroughfare which is true for 80 metres. But then the Salters Road turns L up the side of the trees on the N side of the road, on a much diminished path. There is no SP for this little slot, so look out for it. Beyond the gate at Lint Lands Col, 468m, the track weaves down to a huge sphagnum bog then becomes very indistinct. In other words it disappears. Choose the best line across the bog then aim high, the higher the better. There are a couple of sheep-tracks. Choose the higher and make your way up towards the fence. The fence gradually loses height. Wait until you meet it before you start doing so too – otherwise you will end up climbing out of one of the sikes.

Aim for the black shed when you can see it. Then go through the gate opposite and down over the summit of Nagshead Knowe. Join the main track to Bleakhope at the stell by the next shed. There is no alternative to the ford at the Ainsey Burn, but bear in mind what I said earlier about the ford at the River Breamish. Follow the track to the Bleakhopes. Then, at Low Bleakhope we desert the tarmac again for the climb up to Bleakhope Gap. If it is not too wet you might just make it without getting off. Go over the top, down to the col then on to the summit of Little Dod, 386m

Then you whizz down to the Shank Burn. Malcolm Williams says that it

***Clennell Street & Salters' Road.*** *The author riding down to Davidson's Linn, the classic stream crossing on the Salters' Road. On that day the only one daft enough to try!*

is worth doing the whole loop just to fly down here, and he does. The ford at the burn changes every time you visit. The changes are caused by the loose nature of the bottom, so considerable assessment and appraisal are allowed if you are going to attempt it for the first time. For me it is a case of instant assessment and go for it.

## Shank Burn to Alwinton

At the top of the hill keep R to find the gate. The path through the wood used to be a good test piece because of the ruts. It is a lot easier these days but even now, if you do not start correctly, you will not make it without putting a foot down. Follow the arrows across to, and through the farm. Then stay with the tarmac for nearly 3km. I am never sure whether the snow poles are reassuring or not, and did you notice the Skidoo in the shed at the farm. Perhaps this estate should have been called Bleakhope. TR off the road just before the bridge at Coppath Burn. Aim for the footbridge on the moor, but the ford is usually OK. Then go through the gate and along the lip of the valley towards Old Hazeltonrig. The approach to the ford behind the farm is usually worse than the burn itself. And the climb up to the gate will probably restore all the mud you shed in the water. However, as the road improves considerably from here on, the next ford should do a better and more permanent cleaning job for you, as the road along to Scrainwood is usually quite good. There follows a relatively straight tarmac road all the way to Biddlestone, punctuated by a couple of gates. Then from Biddlestone it is SO again to Clennell. Quit the tarmac prior to Rookland but still go SO through the gates towards Alwinton. On reaching Clennell follow the most obvious route through the buildings, out onto the tarmac and soon back to Alwinton. I have done this route both ways several times but like clockwise best – the uphills are not rideable the other way around.

*__Boulmer.__ The Boulmer ride was always intended as a winter route, reserved for days when it was too silly in the hills. Perhaps there is an element of folly in the lanes too!*

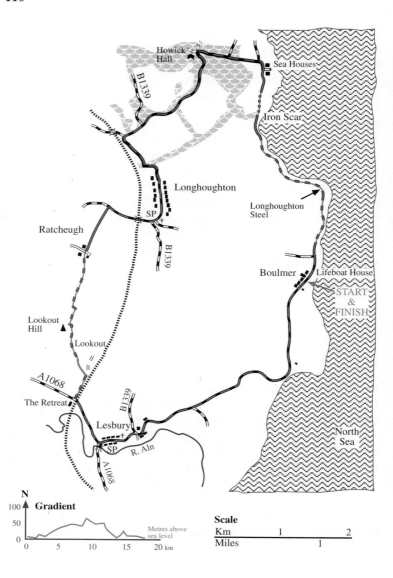

Howick Hall

Sea Houses

B1339

Iron Scar

Longhoughton

Longhoughton Steel

Ratcheugh

SP

B1339

Boulmer

Lifeboat House

Lookout Hill

Lookout

START & FINISH

A1068

The Retreat

B1339

Lesbury

SP

R. Aln

A1068

North Sea

**N**

**Gradient**

100

50

0

Metres above sea level

0    5    10    15    20 km

**Scale**

Km          1                    2

Miles                1

# 18 Boulmer

| | |
|---|---|
| **Grade** | 9 Sporting |
| **17.72 km** | **(11.01 Miles)** |
| **6.37 km** | Farm Road/Track |
| **11.35 km** | Tarmac |
| **High Point:** | Lookout Hill 60m; Lowest: Boulmer Village 4m |
| **Maps:** | Ordnance Survey, Landranger 81 Alnwick; Explorer 332 Alnwick & Amble |
| **Facilities:** | Pub and Grub at Boulmer |

## PLOTTING PLAN

| *START:* | Approach | Map Reference | Depart |
|---|---|---|---|
| Boulmer Lifeboathouse | – | 81/266141 | N |
| Longhoughton Steel | S | 267½152 | N |
| Sea Houses | S | 258½173½ | W |
| Longhoughton | N | 243155 | S |
| Ratcheugh Farm Road | SE | 235½152 | SW |
| Lookout Hill | NNE | 229134 | S |
| A1068 | NNE | 229123 | SE |
| Lesbury | W | 238117 | ENE |
| *FINISH:* | | | |
| Boulmer Lifeboathouse | SW | 266141 | – |

## Route Description

When winter in the hills is just too much, or you need to convince someone that mountain biking really is easy and fun, this is the route. We have had some great winter days following the coast, and I am not unknown to sneak down on a warm day in the summer to remind myself that my chosen pursuit has a mellower side.

The younger members of the family will adore the farm road from Ratcheugh to Lookout because I have never seen it without at least one muddy pool – in fact it usually boasts several. I choose to start at the S end of Boulmer because there is more parking, and you can have a paddle when you finish!

## Boulmer to Longhoughton

Ride N through the village then straight onto the old county road that hugs the coast. There are several gates but it is not a place to hurry. Bird life abounds, and particularly in winter one is frequently rewarded with the unusual. One November afternoon I saw ten curlew in the field opposite Longhoughton Steel, and in rough weather the little bay at Iron Scars seems to attract everything – even herons which are not all that common on the Northumberland coastline. They somehow give the place a Scottish feel. You regain tarmac near Sea Houses farm, then TL onto the main road towards Howick Hall.

The deciduous woodland skirting the road for the next couple of kilometres is always interesting, but bonniest in spring and autumn when the beeches are at their best. It is tarmac all the way to Longhoughton which has heavy military associations. The street names will tell which service.

## Longhoughton to Boulmer

At the S end of the village swing R under the railway bridge. Then TL into the farm road to Ratcheugh. Follow this straight ahead all the way to the A1068 at The Retreat at the N end of the Lesbury viaduct. The farm road is used by big tractors which do not mind a pool or two. Sooner or later a puddle will lure you in. Choose a little one! At Lookout Hill the road jinks L and R through the wall then disappears into a grassy field above Lookout Farm. Keep near to the fence on the R and you will arrive at a wicket gate.

The last field is a bit of a test, but there is a little track among the long grass. Please do not ride on the planted area. When you reach the farm road again TR and run parallel to the railway down to the main road. TL under the bridge, along to Lesbury, and onwards to Boulmer.

***Stob Cross Loop.*** *Allendale Town from the horrendous little hill emanating from Lonkley Terrace. By the time you reach here you've probably done half the climbing involved in the entire route! Five rides start at Allendale which really is the hub of the district.*

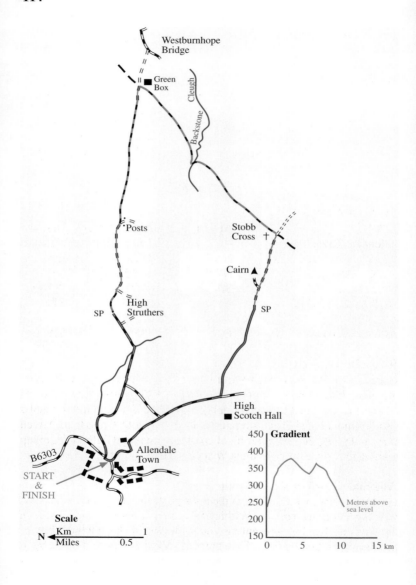

Westburnhope
Bridge

Green
Box

Cleugh

Backstone

Posts

Stobb
Cross †

Cairn ▲

SP

High
Struthers

SP

High
Scotch Hall

B6303

START
&
FINISH

Allendale
Town

**Scale**

N

Km                    1
Miles        0.5

**Gradient**

450
400
350
300
250
200
150

Metres above
sea level

0        5        10        15 km

## 19   Stobb Cross Loop

**Grade**             15 Energetic
**10.32 km**          **(6.41 Miles)**
**5.88 km**           Moorland Track/Path
**1.l 1 km**          Farm/Estate Road
**3.33 km**           Tarmac
**High Points:** Stobb Cross 395m, Long Rigg 363m
**Maps:**             Ordnance Survey, Landranger 87 Hexham & Haltwhistle;
                      Explorer OL43 Hadrian's Wall
**Facilities:**       None on route. Pubs and grub in Allendale Town

### PLOTTING PLAN

| *START:* | **Approach** | **Map Reference** | **Depart** |
|---|---|---|---|
| Allendale Town | – | 87/838$^1$/$_2$558 | SE |
| Scotch Halls Road End | NNW | 845$^1$/$_2$546 | E |
| Stobb Cross | NW | 863$^1$/$_2$539 | NE |
| Green Shed | SW | 881553$^1$/$_2$ | WNW |
| High Struthers Gate | E | 855557 | SW |
| *FINISH:* | | | |
| Allendale Town | E | 839559 | SW |

### Route Description

If this is the first route you try from this guide, I am delighted. This is a mountain bike route in a mountain bike guide. You will need the lowest of those many gears just to get out of Allendale Town, you will need a certain amount of skill and strength to ride from Stobb Cross to the Green Box, and you will need a fair bit of common sense and faith in your map reading to choose the right track W across the moor to finish. Good luck.

### Allendale Town to Stobb Cross

Lonkley Terrace runs SSE from the town centre starting at the offset XR with banks on two corners. Within 200 metres it rears up the hillside in an alarming fashion, presenting you with one of the toughest bits of tarmac in Northumberland. Then there is a second stage to the hill, but it is easy compared with the first. Go on past a little road on the left, then after another 700 metres TL onto an old county road just beyond High Scotch Hall, SP 'Byway for 0.5 mile'. This metalled but broken road leads you directly to the edge of the moor where a SP for Harwood Shield points our way. Keep straight ahead with the main track.

Do not be tempted by the cairn on the top of the hill. You will just have to come down again and have wasted energy. Then on the flattest bit of the moor, you come to Stobb Cross. Keep an eye out for it because the 'Cross' is only a tiny post which bears the bridleway arrows, and is often laid flat by sheep or snow. At this unlikely 'crossroads' we turn L onto a tiny track, which you soon become accustomed to, and head NE to the Green Box.

### Stobb Cross to Allendale Town
Stick with the obvious sheep-track – the surrounding moor might look better but it is not. There is a particularly glutinous 50 metres in the middle of the moor which is rideable if frozen or bone dry, but you will need a fair bit of strength and balance on all other occasions. A technical (loose) descent takes you down to Backstone Cleugh, which might or might not be rideable.

Thereafter, stick fairly close to the wall on the R and follow the track along to the Green Box above Westburnhope Bridge. If you stand with your back to the gate at the box and look W, you should easily identify the track for the final moor crossing. It is a twin track for the first 50 metres past a large stone then becomes a sheep-track for the gentle climb up onto the fell. After 1 km it becomes a Landrover track again, which you follow right across to cultivated land. The final test comes within 250 metres of the edge of the moor. The Landrover track veers L though a gate in the wall but this is not a Right of Way. Our route lies down a bumpy, reedy alternative to the next gate in the corner where you can see a SP. Then it is down in a major way to Allendale Town. Now you are competent you will be able to attack the Stobb Cross Extension. But be warned – not only is it further, it is more difficult too.

**Rothbury Carriage Drive.** Sunday morning. December, remnants of the Simonside Snipes racing team proving they can still ride a bike, but it is not that impressive when they all live within five kilometres of here.

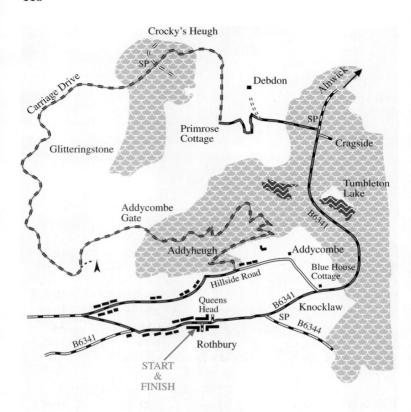

Crocky's Heugh

SP

Carriage Drive

Debdon

Alnwick

Glitteringstone

Primrose Cottage

SP

Cragside

Addycombe Gate

Tumbleton Lake

Addyheugh

Addycombe

B6341

Blue House Cottage

Hillside Road

Queens Head

B6341

Knocklaw

B6341

SP

B6344

Rothbury

START & FINISH

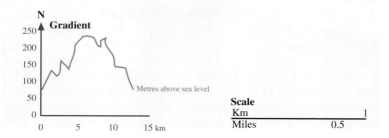

**N**

**Gradient**

250
200
150
100
50
0

Metres above sea level

0    5    10    15 km

**Scale**

Km                                    1

Miles                      0.5

## 20 Rothbury Carriage Drive

| | |
|---|---|
| **Grade** | 14 Energetic |
| **11.55 km** | **(7.80 Miles)** |
| **6.41 km** | Estate Road |
| **0.37 km** | Forest Track/Path |
| **5.77 km** | Tarmac |
| **High Point:** | Carriage Drive above Glitteringstone 247m |
| **Maps:** | Ordnance Survey, Landranger 81, Alnwick & Morpeth; Explorer 332 Alnwick & Amble |
| **Facilities:** | All usual Northumbrian market town facilities in Rothbury. Car parking can be a problem – use the big carpark across the river opposite the Queens Head at 057015 |

### PLOTTING PLAN

| *START:* | Approach | Map Reference | Depart |
|---|---|---|---|
| Queens Head, Rothbury | – | 81/058018 | ENE |
| Debdon Road End | S | 066$\frac{1}{2}$033$\frac{1}{2}$ | W |
| Primrose Cottage Gate | SSE | 059$\frac{1}{2}$034 | NNE |
| Double Gate Crossroads | NE | 054$\frac{1}{2}$038 | SW |
| Carriage Drive | NNE | 045026 | SSE |
| Addycombe Gate | WNW | 054$\frac{1}{2}$025 | SE |
| Adycombe | W | 063$\frac{1}{2}$025 | WSW |
| Hillside Road | NNW | 060$\frac{1}{2}$022 | W |
| Hillside/Pondicherry | NE | 050017 | ESE |
| *FINISH:* | | | |
| Queens Head | SSW | 058018 | – |

### Route Description

Just the thing for a nice day out: entertaining when the ruts are frozen and there are stretches of snow to test your technique; and beautiful on a summer's evening, sitting watching the sun set over the Cheviots, then nipping down into Rothbury for a pint. The route is not very long but its amazing situation affords extensive views to the north, west and south as you ride around. Not only did Lord Armstrong have the greatest industrial brain of his time, but an eye for natural beauty and terrific imagination. This carriage drive, an outrigger of the Cragside Estate, is one of his finest designs. Nothing is for nothing. The climb out of Rothbury to Debdon road end is a bit of a test, especially the last 300m. If you have a companion of lesser physical fitness, give him a chance and convince him it will be worth it. It is.

### Rothbury to Primrose Cottage

The Queens Head is at the E end of Rothbury, a convenient starting point. Follow the main road E out of the town then fork L towards Alnwick on the B6341. The road climbs quite steeply past Knocklaw, then drops a little past Tumbleton Lake before it climbs again to Debdon road end. TL towards Debdon, through the trees which quickly screen the sound of the main road, and within 200 metres you are in the depths of the country. Leave the gate as you find it, then pause for a minute at the farm road junction, and enjoy the view before you zoom downhill to Primrose Cottage. The bridleway we take from the gate opposite the cottage can be seen skirting the wood, climbing steadily then disappearing around behind the trees.

### Primrose Cottage to Addyheugh

The SP opposite the cottage declares 'Bridleway, Crocky's Heugh' which is near Black Pool, but it is only just more than a kilometre in reality. Twice I have seen squashed adders on this track. It is either a favourite basking site or the farm has a fast tractor. This is the Carriage Drive, and all you have to do is follow it right around the hill. When you reach the double gates across the red road go SO, SP Thropton, then climb gently on the compacted road. As the road rises, views unfold. Take your time, stop frequently, and enjoy it. Eventually you will reach the Addycombe gate. Note the little blue bridleway arrow. The final little climb above Addyheugh Crag takes you through a very narrow and pleasant avenue. Watch out for horses and pedestrians. You cannot see very far ahead in places, and due to the herbage the surface is often slippy.

## Addyheugh to Rothbury

Follow the paved carriage drive over the crest of the hill, through the woodland and down – steeply in places – looking to turn hairpin R at the bottom of the zigzags 1.55 km beyond the Addycombe gate. A post with a blue bridleway arrow confirms the turn onto a much lesser track which shrinks, becomes seriously interspersed with boulders and tree roots, and eventually squeezes down a slippery path through rhododendrons. It then swings L in an open area at the end of the houses after a further 0.47 km and sneaks through a 'hole in the hedge' that exits onto Hillside Road. If it's wet, be prepared to 'dab' or even dismount in the latter stages. On reaching Hillside Road TR and follow it all the way to its end, TL and freewheel back down into Rothbury.

***Blanchland Moor.*** *Looking S from the high point on Blanchland Moor over Bulbeck Common and Birkside Fell into County Durham. You use this track in both directions, so any hard work you put in on the outward leg is rewarded in full.*

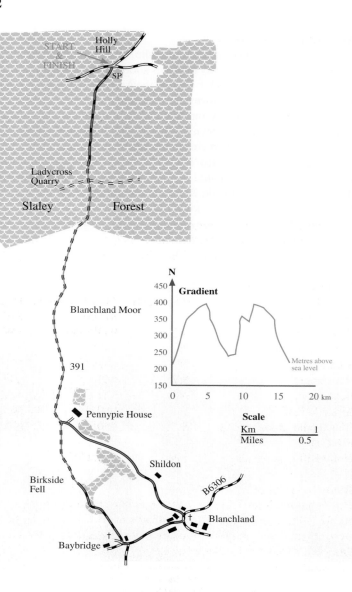

Holly
Hill

START
&
FINISH

SP

Ladycross
Quarry

Slaley          Forest

**N**

Blanchland Moor

450
400
350
300
250
200
150

**Gradient**

Metres above
sea level

391

0     5     10     15     20 km

Pennypie House

**Scale**

| Km | 1 |
| --- | --- |
| Miles | 0.5 |

Birkside
Fell

Shildon

B6306

† Blanchland

†
Baybridge

## 21   Blanchland Moor

| | |
|---|---|
| **Grade** | 15 Energetic |
| **16.09 km** | **(10.00 Miles)** |
| **7.77 km** | Moorland Track |
| **1.42 km** | Forest Road |
| **6.90 km** | Tarmac |
| **High point:** | Blanchland Moor 391m |
| **Maps:** | Ordnance Survey, Landranger 87 Hexham & Haltwhistle; Explorer OL43 Hadrian's Wall |
| **Facilities:** | Tea Rooms, Hotel, Shop in Blanchland |

*Comment: Avoid this route altogether between mid-April and the beginning of June to allow the grouse to nest and hatch undisturbed. Thank you.*

### PLOTTING PLAN

| START: | Approach | Map Reference | Depart |
|---|---|---|---|
| Holly Hill Crossroads | – | 87/958567$^{1}/_{2}$ | SW |
| Forest Edge | NE | 953$^{1}/_{2}$546 | SW |
| Blanchland Moor | N | 950526 | S |
| Shildon | NW | 960510 | SE |
| Blanchland | NW | 965$^{1}/_{2}$503$^{1}/_{2}$ | SW |
| Baybridge | NE | 957$^{1}/_{2}$500$^{1}/_{2}$ | NW |
| Birkside Fell | S | 950514 | N |
| Blanchland Moor | S | 950526 | N |
| FINISH: | | | |
| Holly Hill Crossroads | SW | 958567$^{1}/_{2}$ | – |

### Route Description

This is a route I never tire of. At the height of summer the place turns purple with heather bloom; in the depths of winter it can he brilliant arctic white or so gloomily brooding that you cannot see the Derwent Reservoir barely three miles away.

Strangely, despite its accessibility, I have only ever met one other cyclist, one of the Consett lads out for a Sunday morning run on his tourer – so you can surmise that the surfaces are pretty good, although he was walking when we met him!

Starting at Holly Hill provides a 50 mph downhill finish if you are brave or daft enough. There are also the loose downhills to Pennypie House on both approaches and the flee down into Blanchland on the outward leg. Inevitably there are a couple of climbs too!

## Holly Hill Crossroads to Blanchland
There is a little compressed earth lay-by on the NW corner of Holly Hill crossroads big enough for two cars at a squeeze. Depart SW towards Ladycross, then before you have really got your legs working, you start to climb; gently at first, then steeper and steeper. It is also dead straight and unfortunately you can see what lies ahead. In early autumn you can always get off and pretend to pick the excellent bilberries that grow on the east side of the hill – but you will not, you will make it.

Follow your nose through the forest to the gate on the southern edge. Then you will see the old road stretching away over Blanchland Moor. Most of the track is good, but occasional boggy stretches will really test your power and route-finding skills in the wet season – July to May! The gentle climb onto the high moor is one of the easiest in Northumberland. You become so engrossed with picking a line and surmounting each little bedrock challenge that you gain height painlessly. It is only on the way back, when you are flying down the hill that you realise how steep it was.

The gate at the top of the hill will bring an enforced stop, so take the opportunity to have a look around – it is worth it. The next gate heralds the descent to Pennypie House. It is usually bumpy and fast, but take care in spring when the winter frosts can have made it quite loose. Keep L around the wall at the bottom, through the gate past the farm and downhill all the way to Blanchland. The tarmac beyond Shildon can be busy at weekends in the summer, so take care. When you reach Blanchland TR along to Baybridge.

## Blanchland to Holly Hill

At Baybridge we TR up the steep hill guarded by a 'No Through Road' sign. Would we choose any other? Do not grumble too much at the gradient, it is now comparatively easy, because it is tarmac. Until a couple of years ago it had a loose surface, and that really was a test. Eventually the tarmac ends beyond the summit gate and we head back across the moor on an excellent green road. This is Birkside Fell.

The little ford near Pennypie House can be a bit turbulent in wet weather – treat it with respect. On the other hand, at the height of summer, you will hardly notice it is there. Then it is back up the stony hill onto the moor and across to Slaley Forest.

The final treat is that dreadful hill through the woods; but this time it is in our favour. Just watch out at the caravan site entrance if you are going for the magic 50.

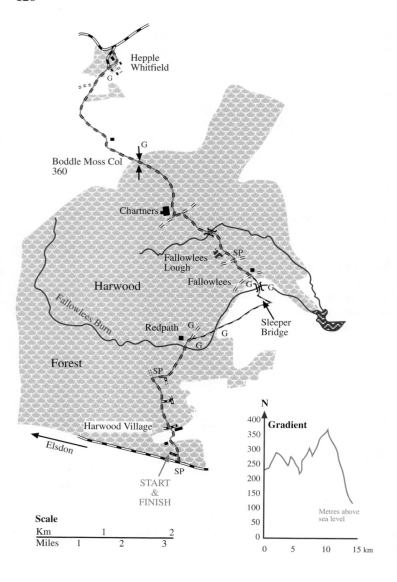

Hepple
Whitfield

G

Boddle Moss Col
360

G

Chartners

Fallowlees
Lough

Fallowlees

Harwood

G   G

Redpath

G

Sleeper
Bridge

G   G

Fallowlees Burn

Forest

SP

Harwood Village

Elsdon

SP

START
&
FINISH

N

**Gradient**

400
350
300
250
200
150
100
50
0

Metres above
sea level

0        5        10        15 km

**Scale**

Km                    1                    2
Miles    1         2         3

# 22 Harwood Forest

| | |
|---|---|
| **Grade** | 13 Energetic |
| **14.00 km** | **(8.7 Miles)** |
| **0.9 km** | Tarmac |
| **6.4 km** | Forest Road |
| **4.3 km** | Farm/Estate Road |
| **1.0 km** | Forest Track/Path |
| **1.3 km** | Moorland Track |
| **High Point:** | Boddle Moss Col 360m |
| **Maps:** | Ordnance Survey, Landranger 81 Alnwick & Morpeth; Explorer OL42 Kielder Water |
| **Facilities:** | None on route. Use signposted 'MTB carpark' off Harwood Village approach road. |

## PLOTTING PLAN

| *START:* | Approach | Map Reference | Depart |
|---|---|---|---|
| Harwood Road End | – | 003898 | NNW |
| Redpath | SSE | 005927 | E |
| Log Bridge | WSW | 011929$^{1}/_{2}$ | ENE |
| Sleeper Bridge | SE | 021937 | NE |
| Fallowlees | SE | 019942$^{1}/_{2}$ | NW |
| Chartners | SE | 001$^{1}/_{2}$957$^{1}/_{2}$ | N |
| Boddle Moss Col | SE | 994970 | W |
| FINISH: | | | |
| Hepple Whitefield Farm | SSE | 987996 | – |

## Route Description

Harwood Village to Hepple Whitefield Farm represents the longest direct bridleway across the western side of the Simonside Hills, and although much of our route might appear to have been created by the Forestry Commission, there have been trade routes across this area of high ground for centuries. In the days of the Scottish wars this was frequently a scene of devastation. In 1297, Wallace with his victorious army ravaged most of Northumberland making Rothbury Forest, which extended from Fallowlees eastwards, his headquarters. Not only were the Scots the enemy, but in 1549 the nightly watch of fifteen or sixteen men were also alert for the raids from Redesdale to the west. All the farmers lived in bastle houses or fortified peles and stock was locked up in the ground floor every night. Inevitably folklore abounds in such an area but my favourite story, concerning Old Will Scott, a well known character who died in 1862, is reputed to be true. It said that Will was perfectly ignorant of the alphabet owing to the high resolve of his father that none of his family should ever be hanged for forgery.

The route passes two very old houses, Fallowlees and Chartners. Fallowlees, currently farmed by the Tinlin family, was once a village but was recorded as a solitary shepherd's house as long ago as 1671. Since then it has survived as a farm. Chartners alas has little land around it and even the little lough mentioned by David Dippie Dixon in his wonderful work 'Upper Coquetdale' has disappeared. Once the home of the lesser yellow water lily, the Nuphar intermedium of Ledebour, a subspecies not known elsewhere in Britain, I suspect it succumbed to modern drainage techniques. Lastly, the downhill from Boddle Moss Col to Hepple Whitefield cuts through a well-managed grouse moor. Please respect the guns, should you arrive on the day of a shoot.

### Harwood to Fallowlees
Start at the end of the tarmac road leading N to Harwood Village. The verges are always cut and make a very pleasant beginning. Jink L and R with the road into the village then bear immediately L and head for the forest, then it is straight ahead for 1.2 km. Follow the SP for Redpath/Fallowlees off to the R and stay on this main forest road for a further 1.3 km. Immediately after crossing the bridge over the Fallowlees Burn at Redpath, TR onto a forest track and make for the rusty gate. This is a rough road, generously endowed with reeds and heather, which gradually shrinks to a challenging deer track. From the gate at the edge of the forest it is 0.62 km to the point where we TR through the trees to cross

Fallowlees Burn . There are two blue 'bridleway' arrows showing a path through the trees. When you reach the burn turn L and follow it downstream to a new bridge which you cross.

From the bridge the route lies straight ahead – 70 metres up the firebreak to the hunting gate at the edge of the forest. Beyond the gate the track rises quite steeply to the rim of the valley. In very dry weather this is rideable – any dampness about, forget it. We now follow the Fallowlees Burn downstream but keep to the highest ground. On gaining the top of the hill, drift across towards the fence on the R. Choose a suitable sheep-track and follow the fence until it ends. Pause in the depression where the fence ends. You can see another bridge, our next objective, about 300 metres ahead – so you know what you are aiming for. Keep high and ride around the rim of the valley again until you reach a little white-topped post and bridleway arrow. Then hairpin L down the old gulley track.

Take care on the bridge. it is used mainly by sheep and extremely slippy when wet. There is also the possibility of a gliff, courtesy of the mallards who regularly nest underneath.

From the bridge follow the track up past the aged hawthorn tree to the gate, through the wood and across the reedy field to Fallowlees. Join the main forest road again going past the W end of the farm. Then go up to the forestry XR where it is SO. Fallowlees Lough is an ideal place to pause; perhaps in the company of a lone heron in winter, or a pair of woodcock on a summer evening. Chartners lies 2 km beyond Fallowlees. We want to go up the hill at the side of the house which can be seen as soon as you reach the junction. You must TL then hairpin R after 170 metres to achieve this.

A further 1.5 km brings us to the edge of the forest, and the gate at Boddle Moss Col. Although one of the windiest spots in the Simonside Hills, it is always worth five minutes spent just gazing at the view over the Coquet valley and into the Cheviots beyond. It is not the best place for lunch but often we don coats and put up with the hurricane simply because of the vista. And it also gives you time to contemplate the excitement to come. Downhill for just over 3 km to the gate at Hepple Whitefield. 2.5km to the wall at the bottom of the steepest bit. Then 60°R at the corner of the wood following the bridleway signs across the field and onto the red road. Enjoy it. Bear L with the road at the big house. Then TR at the bridleway signs on the drive to cross the field to the farm. From the stile at the farm continue straight across between the house and the buildings and around to the tarmac road. If you need to get back to the Start you can reverse the route. An alternative is to TL onto the B6341, and follow this until you come to Elsdon. Go straight through the village and continue on the B6341, over Battle Hill, until you arrive back at Harwood.

***Right: Harwood Forest.** Much of the Harwood route comprises forest road, but there is also a fair percentage of muddy singletrack. Here, Steve Bell proves deceptively fast through the winter leaves - the other shots were all blurred!*

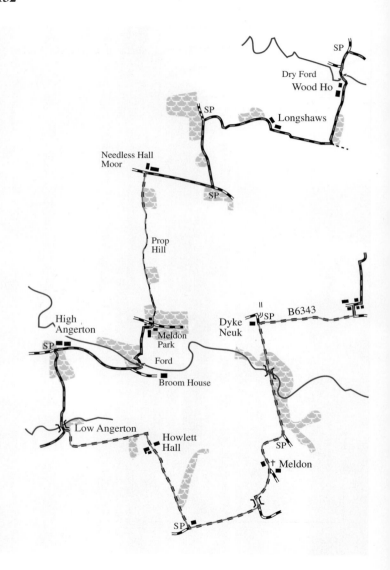

SP

Dry Ford
Wood Ho

SP
Longshaws

Needless Hall
Moor

SP

Prop
Hill

Dyke
Neuk
SP
B6343

High
Angerton

SP
Meldon
Park
Ford

Broom House

Low Angerton
Howlett
Hall

SP
† Meldon

SP

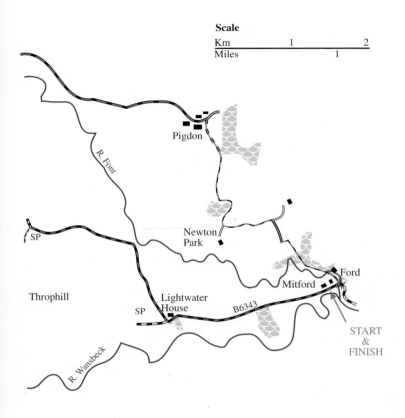

**Scale**

| Km | 1 | 2 |
|---|---|---|
| Miles | | 1 |

R. Font

Pigdon

Newton Park

SP

Throphill

Lightwater House

SP

B6343

Mitford

Ford

START & FINISH

R. Wansbeck

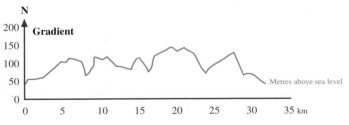

**N**

**Gradient**

Metres above sea level

200
150
100
50
0

0   5   10   15   20   25   30   35 km

## 23 Wansbeck Wanderings

| | |
|---|---|
| **Grade** | 12 Sporting |
| **31.46 km** | **(19.55 Miles)** |
| **16.97 km** | Tarmac |
| **5.09 km** | Farm/Estate Road |
| **9.40 km** | Farm/Field Track |
| **High Point:** | Prop Hill 147m |
| **Maps:** | Ordnance Survey, Landranger 81 Alnwick & Morpeth; Explorer 325 Morpeth & Blyth |
| **Facilities:** | Pub & Grub Plough Inn, Mitford; Dyke Neuk, Meldon Park Corner |

## PLOTTING PLAN

| *START:* | Approach | Map Reference | Depart |
|---|---|---|---|
| Plough Inn, MITFORD | – | 172$^1$/$_2$860$^1$/$_2$ | SW |
| Lightwater House | ESE | 149856 | NNW |
| Nunriding Corner | ESE | 133868 | SSW |
| Throphill | N | 130$^1$/$_2$857 | W |
| Dyke Neuk | ESE | 118$^1$/$_2$856$^1$/$_2$ | SSE |
| Meldon | NNW | 119837 | SSW |
| Meldon Lane House | ENE | 109$^1$/$_2$829 | NNW |
| Low Angerton | SE | 093$^1$/$_2$842$^1$/$_2$ | NNW |
| High Angerton | SSE | 092853 | NE |
| Meldon Park | WSW | 105856 | N |
| Needless Hall Moor | S | 103$^1$/$_2$877 | ESE |
| Longshaws Road End | S | 111883$^1$/$_2$ | E |
| Stanton Road End | SSW | 130892$^1$/$_2$ | ESE |
| Pigdon | W | 156882 | S |
| Newton Park Corner | N | 158$^1$/$_2$868$^1$/$_2$ | E |
| Tree Lined Lonnen | SW | 164$^1$/$_2$869 | SSE |
| *FINISH:* | | | |
| Mitford Bridge/Plough | NNW | 172$^1$/$_2$860$^1$/$_2$ | – |

## Route Description

This route was originally put together to demonstrate the enormous differences in terrain that a line marked on the map as a bridleway can actually present on the ground – but I have fallen in love with it. The surfaces vary from a good, made-up farm road W of Longshaws to a fight down the side of a field between Pigdon and Newton Park. The final slither down to Mitford Dean at the end is your test piece. See if you can ride it without putting your foot down! It is a beautiful run around at any time of the year, despite the fact that wet weather can make many stretches very clarty (muddy to many folk, but in this part of Northumberland it is clarty) – sticky, glutinous, affectionate, and enough to test any washing machine. Wildlife abounds. Approaches by bike are quieter than feet and it is amazing what you will see. One November afternoon I stopped on the bridge over the Wansbeck N of Meldon when a kingfisher flew through the arch. While I was checking the maps a red squirrel bounded across the far end of the bridge, then as I was taking a photograph, a gorgeous dipper flew straight up the river and passed within metres of me. Weasels and stoats are common, and you may see mink.

### Mitford to Meldon Park

Leave the delights of the Plough until you return, otherwise you might never make a start. Go up the hill away from the pub and follow the B6343 W to Lightwater House 2.5 km away. Then we TR towards Nunriding Hall. The next 2 km are little more than a lane and a very pleasant byway. Then at Nunriding corner, we TL through the gate into the field and onto the bridleway to Throphill. The track up the side of the field sees some use by horses and can be a bit lumpy, but you soon reach the end of the lonnen by the power pole that will take you to Throphill. Although quite short, this is a classic country lonnen. Enclosed by hedges, it has two good ruts and a tremendous selection of flora and birdlife. Even in the driest weather there are a few holes that hang onto the water, and in winter the noise you make crunching through the ice is enough to wake the dead on a still day.

When you reach Throphill go through the farmyard and TL through the buildings down to the main road. TJTR when you reach the B6343 again and W to the Dyke Neuk. TL before the pub, through Meldon then TR towards Bolam. TR again at Meldon Lane House through the gate to Howlett Hall. Take your time *en route* to Howlett Hall and you can see most of your route laid out before you. You cannot tell from the map but, as soon as you pass dirough the farm, the road changes dramatically. Tarmac gives way to field road, and it remains as such all the way to Low Angerton several gates later. A very interesting ride. There is a collie at Low Angerton that will chase and nip the last man if given the chance. Watch him.

Head N to High Angerton along one of the bonniest bits of road in the county, then TJTR in the trees and through the farm. Occasionally they have ferrets for sale – just the thing to take home in your bum bag! Follow the estate road E above the river nearly as far as Broom House, which you might have noticed across the fields from Howlett Hall if the sun was bright. Fork L through a gate and down to the paved ford. There are a couple of holes in the bed of the ford where some of the blocks are missing. With concentration it is rideable, although I must admit that in summer I tend to charge at it and often come to grief, whereas in winter I am usually slow and successful. There is, of course, the bridge! A steep track takes you up to Meldon Park. Go straight across the concrete at the first building and the lane will take you around to the main road, and the correct place to go straight across onto the next bridleway.

**Meldon Park to Mitford**
The SP says Needless Hall Moor. It is nearly a straight line N. Initially, cross the W end of the parkland to a gate at a little wood. Cross the fence onto the track and continue N. Follow your nose. There are a couple of places up the side of the woods where horses have not done us any favours but, unless it is very wet, it should be rideable. There is a great view N to the Simonside Hills; the classic silhouette, when the light is fading, from the ridge of Prop Hill. Then good, firm farm road to Needless Hall Moor.

TR onto the tarmac then TL towards Netherwitton after exactly 1 km, to

***Wansbeck Wanderings.*** *Please note it is not compulsory to climb onto the old Wanney's Line which follows much of the Wansbeck valley. Names withheld to avoid public alarm about the medical profession.*

***Stob Cross Extension.*** *The expert approach to water. Emma Guy and Adrian Gidney in their element.*

take us N to Longshaws. The road to the farm is good, and it is probably not too bad afterwards either but, for some reason, it attracts water. The resultant clarts are a local legend. I have never seen it completely dry, but it is great all the same – a good test of technique. Beyond Wood House you can always dip your bike in the river at the dry ford. This is the River Font, the main tributary of the Wansbeck. We re-cross it within 200 metres of the pub.

Go SO onto the tarmac at the top of the hill, TR at Stanton road end and stay on this road all the way to Pigdon. You use the lane that skirts the big house, literally past the garage doors where the 'main' road bears L in the trees. Arrival at the gate at the end of the little lane after 0.16 km will confirm that you made the right choice. The track around the edge of the field swings gently L, but stop when you reach the next gate. Do not go through. Our next gate is down the hedge on the R. There is no track to it. After you get through keep close to the hedge and see if you can ride it. Invariably crops are planted right up to the edge and there is not much room, but it is passable. At the far end of the field there is a wicket gate into a meadow. The bridleway runs around the E side of the wood, so TL then make your way to the corner of the wood and cross the stream by the fallen tree. Hug the wood and the hedge and you will arrive at the galvanised gate at Newton Park corner.

TL onto the last stretch of tarmac along to the point where we TR onto a tree lined lonnen that will take us back to Mitford. It is a skinny little lane, seldom used by the tractors. The horses have made a path down the middle but usually the best traction is available in the grassy ruts on either side. When you reach the gate TL along the avenue of trees and skirt the field to the clarty lonnen leading down to the gate at the bridge. The lonnen is leafy, lumpy and deeply rutted – the sting in the tail. At the bottom TL across the little bridge, up through the farm, then down to the ford. This track will bring you out at Mitford bridge. The Plough is on your right.

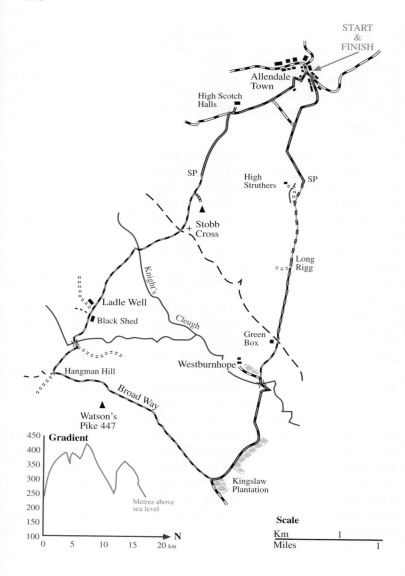

START & FINISH

Allendale Town

High Scotch Halls

SP

High Struthers

SP

Stobb Cross

Long Rigg

Knight's

Cleugh

Ladle Well

Black Shed

Green Box

Westburnhope

Hangman Hill

Broad Way

Watson's Pike 447

Kingslaw Plantation

Gradient

450
400
350
300
250
200
150
100

Metres above sea level

N

0    5    10    15    20 km

Scale

Km        1
Miles        1

## 24 Stobb Cross Extension

| | |
|---|---|
| **Grade** | 16 Energetic |
| **16.87 km** | **(10.48 Miles)** |
| **8.58 km** | Moorland Track/Path |
| **2.95 km** | Farm/Estate Road |
| **5.34 km** | Tarmac |
| **High Points:** | Stobb Cross 395m, Broad Way 425m, Long Rigg 363m |
| **Maps:** | Ordnance Survey, Landranger 87 Hexham & Haltwhistle Explorer OL43 Hadrian's Wall |
| **Facilities:** | None on route. Pubs and grub in Allendale Town |

### PLOTTING PLAN

| *START:* | Approach | Map Reference | Depart |
|---|---|---|---|
| Allendale Town | – | 87/838$^1$/$_2$558 | SE |
| Scotch Halls Road End | NNW | 845$^1$/$_2$546 | E |
| Stobb Cross | NW | 863$^1$/$_2$539 | SE |
| Hangman Hill | NW | 886520$^1$/$_2$ | N |
| Kingslaw Plantation | SW | 902543 | NW |
| Green Box | SE | 881553 | WNW |
| High Struthers Gate | E | 855557 | SW |
| *FINISH:* | | | |
| Allendale Town | E | 839559 | SW |

### Route Description

This is a logical progression from the Stobb Cross Loop, but is a good route in its own right. The going is invariably softer immediately beyond Stobb Cross itself, but the inclusion of a stretch of the Broad Way makes the route. It is narrow, technical, a bit of a toil to begin with, but the gradual downhill section from Watson's Pike to Kingslaw Plantation is one of my all time favourites.

## Allendale Town to Hangman Hill

Depart SE from Allendale Town up Lonkley Terrace. It is worthwhile riding around the market place a few times to warm up for it. If you are cold it just is not funny. Both stages of the hill earn single arrows on the O.S. 1:50,000 map denoting a gradient of between 1 in 7 to 1 in 5 – but how the first bit does not rate three arrows, I do not know. See what you think. Climb onwards and upwards to TL just beyond High Scotch Hall after 1.46 km. Then it is straight ahead all the way to Ladle Well some 3.8 km across the moors.

Initially the old county road is reasonably surfaced if a bit wet in places. But beyond the gate where the SP points us in the direction of Harwood Shield, it becomes softer and more demanding. Do not be tempted by the cairn on the top of the knoll. Keep SO to Stobb Cross. The little post which marks the 'cross' may or may not be standing. As you will appreciate, it is the only thing that even hints that it may resemble a tree in this part of the moor, and the sheep love it to destruction! Go SO and keep R of the wall. Try to keep to the track. Eventually the track becomes narrow and firm again and presents you with a steep descent to Knight's Cleugh. Then there is a loose climb back up onto a good moorland section across to The Drag, an old private grouse road, at Ladle Well. There are several springs in the vicinity which are capped and tapped, the green shed housing the reservoir controls. TL down past the Black Sheds, then R onto a newer grouse road immediately after crossing the bridge at the corner. Trip your computer and watch out for the "XR" 0.56 km up this road on Hangman Hill. You arrive at a slight dip in the road which is reinforced by a couple of railway sleepers, the only other marker being a small pile of stones. Do not be lured on by the grouse road – it ceases another 500 metres farther on in the middle of Lilswood Moor.

## Hangman Hill to Allendale Town

You might wonder how the skinny little track we now join and head N, could be called Broad Way. The simple answer is that its days as a packhorse route and ancient thoroughfare are long gone. But in places you will see the troughs of erosion caused by hooves many years ago. Today it is an excellent moorland bridleway climbing initially up the western flank of Watson's Pike, then down, down, and technically down, as it weaves its way through the heather over 3 km to Kingslaw Plantation. It really is good. TL at the Plantation corner for a tarmac flee down to Westburnhope Bridge. Then TR through the gate to climb another old and waterworn county road to the Green Box. Beyond the gate at the Green Box, go as straight ahead as you can and head W across the moor on a single sheep-track. Our route grows again at the white-tipped posts after 1 km. Apart from one place where we cut off a corner, we follow this all the way back to enclosed farmland. The grouse road turns L through the wall near High Struthers, but we need to fight our way down a reedy twin-track to the SP 240 metres away in the corner. This is the last test. Thereafter it is SO with the tarmac all the way down into Allendale Town.

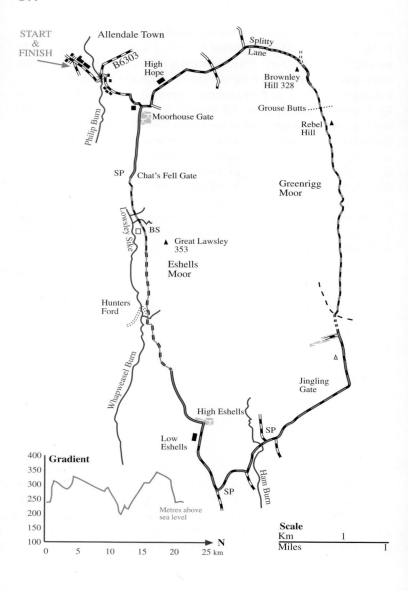

START & FINISH

Allendale Town

Splitty Lane

B6303

High Hope

Brownley Hill 328

Philip Burn

Moorhouse Gate

Grouse Butts

Rebel Hill

Greenrigg Moor

SP Chat's Fell Gate

Lowsley Sike

BS

Great Lawsley 353

Eshells Moor

Hunters Ford

Whapweasel Burn

Jingling Gate

High Eshells

SP

Low Eshells

SP

Ham Burn

**Gradient**

400
350
300
250
200
150
100

Metres above sea level

0    5    10    15    20    25 km

N

**Scale**
Km                    1
Miles                        1

# 25 Moors of Greenrigg & Eshells

| | |
|---|---|
| **Grade** | 17 Strenuous |
| **20.89 km** | **(12.98 Miles)** |
| **8.91 km** | Moorland Track/Path |
| **2.7 km** | Farm Road |
| **9.28 km** | Tarmac |
| **High Points:** | Brownley Hill 328m, Near Great Lawsley 343m |
| **Maps:** | Ordnance Survey, Landranger 87 Hexham & Haltwhistle; Explorer OL43 Hadrian's Wall |
| **Facilities:** | None on route. Pubs, grub and tearooms in Allendale Town |

## PLOTTING PLAN

| *START:* | Approach | Map Reference | Depart |
|---|---|---|---|
| Allendale Town Market Place | – | 87/838½558½ | NE |
| Moorhouse Gate | S | 845½568 | N |
| Splitty Lane End | S | 836½585 | N |
| Rebel Hill | WSW | 848595 | ENE |
| Triangulation Pillar 291 | WSW | 887598 | ENE |
| Ham Burn | NW | 901586 | SE |
| Eshells Moor | E | 898578 | W |
| Moorhouse Gate | E | 845½568 | S |
| *FINISH:* | | | |
| Allendale Town Market Place | NE | 838½558½ | – |

## Route Description

To like this one you have to like moors. There is next to no cover once you commit yourself to the crossings and you could find yourself lying in a hollow to get out of the wind while you grab a snack. Despite the exposure this is one of my favourite loops: rough, tough, and invariably wet; one finds oneself flying over testing terrain on Greenrigg Moor if there is even a hint of a westerly wind; and then stooped in effort often into a moisture-laden gale on the return journey across Eshells, reminding oneself 'this is what it is all about'. About two o'clock in the afternoon one day very early in November – having crunched my way across both legs of the tour in some of the first serious ice of the winter; been smitten by snowflakes to the point where I could not see very well through my clear glasses but did not dare take them off; and having pedalled the whole of Eshells Moor in low gears – I returned to the farm at Moorhouse Gate just in time to meet the shepherd bringing the sheep down off the hill. I congratulated myself on having made it then shot down to the Allendale Tea Rooms to recuperate. But it is not always like this. Sit quietly on the side of Great Lawsley on a summer afternoon listening to the grouse remonstrating "Go back, back, back, back, back" and there are few better places in the country.

### Allendale Town to jingling Gate

Ride NE on the B6303 away from the Market Place then TR steeply uphill immediately after you cross the bridge over Philip Burn. This bank always kills me, I only hope you fare better. Eventually you reach the junction at the trees at Moorhouse Gate. This is where you return to. But on the outward leg we go SO then TL 140 metres farther on to pass the aptly named High Hope. The view of East Allen Dale from up here is great, so have a look around when you pause to check the map. The first taste of loose comes with Splitty Lane End. I wish I could explain the name, but cannot. This takes you up to the very edge of the moor and a splendid track signposted Rebel Hill. Follow the wall only for the first 100 metres. Then go SO onto a lesser track when the tractor ruts turn R, and climb steadily to the little summit of Brownley Hill, 328m. Soon after, we bear R onto a better defined track as directed by the little bridleway arrow. This is the track we follow right across Greenrigg Moor. The quality and definition varies considerably and there is even one section where the track wanders quite considerably from the line of the bridleway drawn on the map. But keep faith and weave around the enclosure in the middle of the moor. You should ultimately aim for the extreme right end of the wall that declares more controlled pasture. The sting in the tail comes as you round the end of the wall. Even in the driest summer there is water here, but it would not be a good route without a challenge or two. Tarmac now takes you past the triangulation pillar to Jingling Gate corner and S to the Ham Burn.

## Ham Burn to Allendale Town

After crossing the Ham Burn you simply TR then R again to pass through Low and High Eshells. Re-cross the heath, this time using Eshells Moor. More obviously a grouse moor, the track is better defined, but not necessarily easier – in fact it is quite difficult in wet weather. Rule One applies: 'Do what you think is best!' Four-wheel drive vehicles have carved more than one track but basically head W and N of the Whapweasel Burn – surely the most gloriously named watercourse in the shire. Near the Hunter's Ford our track follows the line of the shooting butts. It then wiggles L and R through the white-topped posts to a mini-ford above the actual Hunter's version. The track nearest the Lawsley Sike is usually the best, even if you are forced to ride on the elevated central section. Beyond the boundary stone in the western section, the track diminishes considerably. There are little dykes to hop, rushes to negotiate, and sphagnum stoppers to test your strength. Keep W and head for Chat's Fell Gate. The final stanza comprises a dash down between stony walls on an equally stony track to Moorhouse Gate. Then flee down that horrendous hill into Allendale. Enjoy it.

***Moors of Greenrigg & Eshells.*** *Splitty Lane End, start of the roughstuff across Greenrigg Moor, simply follow the singletrack up and across the 'white ground'. New 'Grouse Roads' have been built, but few coincide with the bridleways.*

**Vallum.** *The niceties of the Vallum long forgotten, this is the bridleway across Butt Rigg- the trees have probably grown a bit since this picture was taken. We can only hope that the forestry vehicles have flattened the tracks a bit too!*

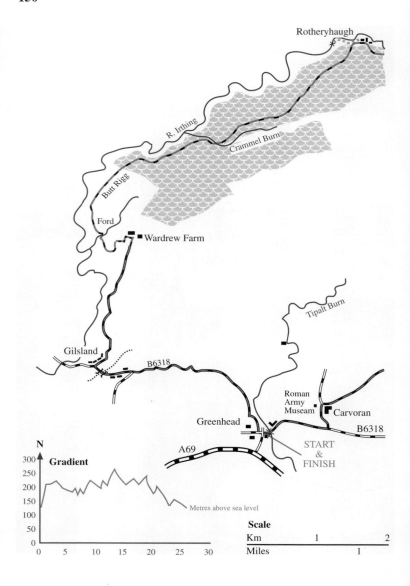

Rotheryhaugh

R. Irthing

Crammel Burn

Butt Rigg

Ford

Wardrew Farm

Tipalt Burn

Gilsland

B6318

Roman
Army
Museam

Carvoran

Greenhead

B6318

A69

START
&
FINISH

**N**

**Gradient**

300
250
200
150
100
50
0

Metres above sea level

0    5    10    15    20    25    30

**Scale**

Km          1          2

Miles              1

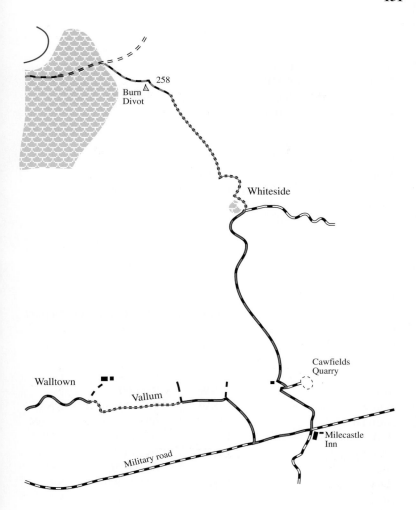

258
Burn
Divot

Whiteside

Cawfields
Quarry

Walltown

Vallum

Milecastle
Inn

Military road

## 26 Vallum

| | |
|---|---|
| **Grade** | 19 Strenuous |
| **25.56 km** | **(15.88 Miles)** |
| **3.63 km** | Moorland Track/Path |
| **4.55 km** | Forest Track/Path |
| **2.89 km** | Farm Road |
| **13.89 km** | Tarmac |
| **High Point:** | Burn Divot 258m |
| **Maps:** | Ordnance Survey, Landranger 86 Haltwhistle & Bewcastle; Explorer OL43 Hadrian's Wall |
| **Facilities:** | YHA, pub in Greenhead; pubs, shops, garage in Gilsland |

## PLOTTING PLAN

| *START:* | Approach | Map Reference | Depart |
|---|---|---|---|
| Greenhead Youth Hostel | – | 86/659$\frac{1}{2}$654 | E |
| Greenhead Banktop | WNW | 669655 | NNW |
| Carvoran | S | 668658 | E |
| Vallum | W | 695664 | E |
| Milecastle Inn | WSW | 716660 | N |
| Whiteside Road End | WSW | 707690 | NNW |
| Burn Divot | SE | 694708 | WNW |
| Rotheryhaugh | E | 673$\frac{1}{2}$711 | SSW |
| Crammel Burn | ENE | 654$\frac{1}{2}$696$\frac{1}{2}$ | WSW |
| Gate in Wall | NE | 636687$\frac{1}{2}$ | SSE |
| Wardrew Farm | WNW | 641$\frac{1}{2}$682$\frac{1}{2}$ | SSW |
| B6318 Gilsland | NE | 636$\frac{1}{2}$664 | SE |
| Greenhead | NNW | 659654 | E |
| *FINISH:* | | | |
| Greenhead YHA | W | 659$\frac{1}{2}$654 | – |

## Route Description

How do you fancy a really horrendous day out? How much do you like walking? How high is your determination rating? Little short of an apology is required for including this route if the weather is foul, but to the lover of remote places the rewards are high. Geographically the location is not too wild, but the feeling of space and isolation in the high moors of the Roman Wall is something to be experienced. You are not going to get lost, but you might think you are! And it is absolutely imperative that you take an O.S. map – preferably the Explorer because it has some of the forest roads marked. When you plot the route on your map you will see that we traverse the Vallum, which was a wall of sods and earth set some distance behind Hadrian's Wall. You will see the ditch and raised ramparts stretching away into the distance, especially in the winter when the sun is low, but not all of it is rideable. We use the best 'off-road' stretch. The B6318 Military Road has grabbed the tarmac sections further E. A vallar or vallary was the name given to a crown bestowed in ancient Rome on the first soldier to mount the enemy's rampart. You may feel that you deserve something of that nature on completion of the route. I will just have to design and make badges available for this one! It would also help others to identify the lunatic fringe of mountain biking!

### Greenhead to Whiteside

Depart E up Greenhead Bank on the B6318. TL just over the top where the SP says 'Hadrian's Wall', then TR opposite the Roman Army Museum towards Walltown. Due to the nature of the surrounding land you may think that much of this road is unmade – but actually there is tarmac underneath, although those making a summer tour may wonder what on earth I am talking about when the mud assumes reasonable proportions. Soon after passing a good limekiln on the L we cross a cattle grid and go SO onto an unsurfaced road which leads us to the Vallum. There are a few gates. You simply follow it E until it turns R up to the Military Road. Enjoy a little bit of history by riding along one of the oldest constructed thoroughfares in the land – not a lot different in surface, I imagine, from when it was built. When you reach the Military Road TL but take care, it is dead straight and the traffic whistles along. It is 800 metres to the next XR at the Milecastle Inn where we TL towards Whiteside. We cross the Vallum near Cawfields Quarry where The Wall and the Vallum nearly coincide. Then TL over a little bridge that is easy to miss, and wiggle away N onto the open commons. Whiteside Farm is painted white, and even before you turn off you can see the obvious old road winding its way up past the farm. The testing terrain starts here.

## Whiteside to Greenhead

Bear R in front of the grey shed at Whiteside and follow the old road uphill with the wall. Stick with the main track – the surrounding ground is soft and the farmer is constantly adding material to the road to maintain it. Even the flat bits are lumpy. The ruin on the far ridge is Burn Divot, the highest point on the route. The Landranger map merely shows it as a triangulation pillar, but as you will see it has been a substantial homestead, recorded in old documents as Burn Deviot, said to be haunted, and a resort of smugglers and sheep stealers. All you have to do is aim for it! The bridleway goes around the N side of Burn Divot then WNW across the L side of the next hillock to the forest edge. See if you can find the triangulation pillar. Keep faith with your navigation and you will see the gate onto the forest road as soon as you crest the rise. The best you can hope for in the way of a track is a mark left by the shepherd's quad. Riding up the forest road over a sheet of frozen snow, the Porcupine on my front wheel was making enough noise to wake a mosstrooper, then the going became very difficult. The road had ended and all that remained was the space between the trees – tussocky and wet.

You will have glimpsed the deserted farm of Rotheryhaugh from Burn Divot. Soon you will be able to see it down a ride on the R. Pick the best deer-track and head towards it. A gate in the fence manifests itself, then there are a couple of really ancient gateposts and a hazardous sleeper bridge before you reach the farm. Follow the track W out of the farm and through the paddock gate. Then TL through another gate which is set back a little, before you reach the open grazing by the river, and head SSW up another wide, rough gap between the trees. The only hint of a path is a faint mark as if the shepherd rides through once a year on his motor-bike, or the deer use it from time to time. I praised the snow because it filled the little gulley and made it easier to pick out. It is not straight and it is a constant search to find the line – this continues for 3.1 km. In early summer it might be rideable, but the giant tussocks make it a constant test. You can relate the shape of the mapped bridleway to the forestry rides, but I was still delighted to see the ancient gate on the far side of the Crammel Burn after 2.27 km, which confirmed my navigation. You will often find gates on the line of bridleways long after the track has become overgrown, and this is a fine example. From this point on you keep finding them, which is a great boost when you are tired, so just keep linking them up and adjusting your line accordingly. This ancient gate, at MR 654$\frac{1}{2}$ 696$\frac{1}{2}$, is so old and low it is nearly overgrown with grass. It sports an amazing colony of lichens, but is a great marker. Climb up the hill beyond it, bearing R all the time. Contour around the rim of the valley then swing L up a wider ride past the fire beaters and you should be able to see the next gate – a little metal wicket, near the top of the hill.

Only 140 metres farther on you gain the ridge of Butt Rigg and a rideable track along the top. The first markers are thick posts, then beyond the dip there is another gate in the wall leading to reedy moorland. Contour around again never straying too far from the fence on the R and eventually there is another gate. From here aim across the grassland to a house rooftop – not the farm which is our eventual destination. Then, from the galvanised gate, head for the tall conifers which will lead you down to the ford. Beyond the ford there is a recognisable track again which we follow around Wardrew Farm, and the end of the difficulties. Turn R in the farmyard and flee down to Gilsland. Turn L at the B6318 in the village, under the railway bridge, and twiddle along to Greenhead. There is a ford behind the youth hostel if you need to knock the worst of the mud off your bike, although there is the slimmest of chances you may not have attracted any! Great, wasn't it?

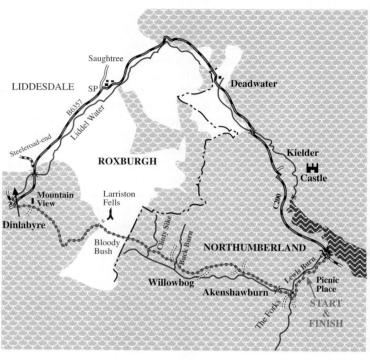

Saughtree
LIDDESDALE
SP
B6357
Liddel Water
Steeleroad-end
**ROXBURGH**
Mountain View
Dinlabyre
Larriston Fells
Bloody Bush
Clinty Sike
Buck Burn
**Deadwater**
**Kielder**
**Castle**
C200
**NORTHUMBERLAND**
Willowbog
Akenshawburn
The Forks
Lewis Burn
Picnic Place
**START & FINISH**

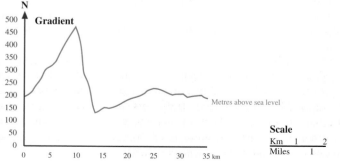

**N**

**Gradient**

500
450
400
350
300
250
200
150
100
50
0

Metres above sea level

0    5    10    15    20    25    30    35 km

**Scale**

Km    1         2
Miles        1

## 27 Bloody Bush Toll Road

| | |
|---|---|
| **Grade** | 14 Energetic |
| **34.95 km** | **(21.72 Miles)** |
| **1.27 km** | Moorland Track/Path |
| **13.29 km** | Forest Track |
| **20.39 km** | Tarmac |
| **High Point:** | Larriston Fells 466m |
| **Maps:** | Ordnance Survey, Landrangers 79 Hawick & Eskdale, 80 Cheviot Hills & Kielder Water; Explorer OL42 Kielder Water |
| **Facilities:** | Toilets at Lewis Burn. Shop at Kielder Village |

## PLOTTING PLAN

| *START:* | Approach | Map Reference | Depart |
|---|---|---|---|
| Lewis Burn Picnic Place | – | 80/636896 | SW |
| The Forks | NE | 630888 | NW |
| Bloody Bush | ESE | 571910 | WNW |
| Dinlabyre | ENE | 79/529921 | NE |
| Steeleroad-end | S | 536½936 | NNE |
| Saughtree | S | 80/561967 | SE |
| Deadwater | N | 604½969 | S |
| Kielder | NNW | 627934 | SSE |
| Lewis Burn | NW | 645903 | W |
| *FINISH:* | | | |
| Lewis Burn Picnic Place | NE | 636896 | – |

## Route Description

It would be a gross understatement to say that one simply hopped over the hill from Lewis Burn to Dinlabyre, then returned via the road passing Saughtree and Kielder Village to fulfill this route – but that is basically what you do. Fortunately, there is a lot more to it. Early in the nineteenth century there was a rash of coalmines, or more correctly, short adit mines or groups of bell-pit workings in the Kielder area. The road network was very poor and in an effort to create employment, and no doubt to make a little money for himself, Sir John Swinburne commissioned the great civil engineer, Thomas Telford to survey a line for a road from Lewisburn Colliery across the border to Dinlabyre on the Scottish side. In 1826 it was estimated that the workable seam at Lewisburn would yield about 10,000 cartloads of household coal and approximately 5,000 cardoads suitable for the limekilns in the Hawick, Castleton and Jedburgh districts. This was an attractive market and the road was started in 1830. Sir John bore the expense of construction but levied tolls which were collected by the keeper at a Toll House at Oakenshaw (now Akenshawburn). It was even hoped that the thoroughfare would eventually become the Great London Road and a route for mail coaches. Also, where the road crossed the border, an inn for travellers and carters was planned. As far as I know, the inn was never built but the huge toll pillar remains.

This is a route I would recommend for folk who are fit enough to do a fair mileage, but perhaps are new to mountain biking. It is a good loop to get the feel of the bike and see what it will do.

### Lewis Burn to Dinlabyre

On leaving Lewisburn Picnic Place continue to head SW into the forest on a good firm road. This is the main thoroughfare in this part of the forest, marked on the Explorer map as Bloody Bush Road. Follow it past The Forks, Akenshawburn and Willowbog all the way to Bloody Bush. Don't fork L at Willowbog, map ref. 601899 – this is the Cross Border Route, number 31. Beyond the Buck Burn, where the new main road sweeps R, the Bloody Bush Road becomes the lesser option. It then reverts to an ancient grassy track before finally becoming a squelchy, reedy lonnen for the last 300 metres to the border and the toll pillar.

Unfortunately, the old bridge over the Clinty Sike has been pulled down. It was in a state of major disrepair, the apex of the arch having deteriorated to only a couple of feet wide – one of the most delicate challenges of this route. Alas, no more. I suppose demolition was the most sensible option, but I miss it. The inscription on the pillar reads:

The MARCH between
NORTHUMBERLAND &
ROXBURGHSHIRE

| Willowbog the | Dinlabyre the |
|---|---|
| Property of Sir | Property of |
| J. E. SWINBURN | William Oliver |
| Bart. CAPHEATON | RUTHERFORD Esq. |

Private road upon which a Toll Gate is erected near Oakenshaw Bridge at which the following Toll rates are exacted

| VIZ | 1st For Horses employed in leading coals | 2d | each |
|---|---|---|---|
| 2nd | all other horses | 3d | do |
| 3rd | cattle | ld | do |
| 4th | sheep, calves, swine | $^1/_2$ | |

The above tolls exacted once a day. NB Persons evading or refusing to pay at the above mentioned toll gate will be prosecuted for trespass.

DISTANCE from this place
BLOODY BUSH

| to Lewisburn Colliery | 5 miles | |
|---|---|---|
| Mounces | 8 | do |
| Bellingham | 23 | - |
| Hexham | 37 | - |
| Dinlabyre | $3^1/_2$ | - |
| Castleton | $7^1/_2$ | - |
| Hawick | 21 | - |
| Jedburgh | 25 | - |

If you are lucky you may see the Cheviot goats near the pillar. It is one of their favourite haunts, but I am usually so intent on trying to ride the last 100 metres to the gate, my noise often frightens them off. From the pillar across to the edge of the Larriston Fells is the toughest part of the route. Invariably reedy and wet, it is on the verge of rideability. In autumn after a good summer's growth, the vegetation can be quite a challenge. It is generally a lot easier in the spring when the shepherd has been across a few times on his motor-bike and carved a bit of a track. We rejoin the forestry road just S of the radio mast for the hurtle down to Dinlabyre. Sometimes the barrier near Mountain View is down so take care in the latter stages.

## Dinlabyre to Lewisburn

Tarmac it might be, but dull it is not. TR onto the B6357 and follow it to Saughtree. En route you pass Steeleroad-end. A glance at the map will reveal the reason for the name Steele Road. The now defunct Waverley Line which ran through Liddesdale on its way to Edinburgh wound up to Riccarton junction where it joined the old North Tyne Railway and then back across to Kielder, the same way we are going. What a brilliant mountain bike route it would have made.

On reaching Saughtree TR for Kielder still following the Liddel Water. Wind your way back into England at Deadwater. An interesting test on a hot day is to try to ride through the tunnel underneath the railway near the cattle grid. You will need a hot day because you are sure to get wet! If you have got time the Forestry Museum at Kielder Castle is worth a visit, then you will know what to look out for on your next ride. You are much quieter awheel than afoot and more likely to see the wildlife.

South of Kielder Village the new C200 seems like a motorway around the lake. Then, after 4 km TR again into the forest to finish back at Lewisburn. On the autumn day when I measured this route a merganser raced me up the Lewis Burn from the road to the picnic place just after sunset – so cool, so quiet, the perfect way to end a mountain bike ride.

---

*Right: Bloody Bush Toll Road. Bloody Bush. The enormous pillar bearing the toll charges marks the border between Scotland and England. It also marks the wettest bit of the route. Enjoy it.*

**162**

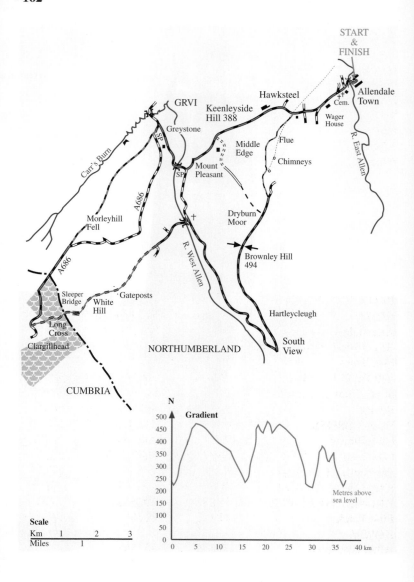

START & FINISH

Allendale Town

Hawksteel

Keenleyside Hill 388

GRVI

Greystone

Cem.

Wager House

R. East Allen

Middle Edge

Flue

Chimneys

Carr's Burn

SP

SP

Mount Pleasant

A686

Morleyhill Fell

Dryburn Moor

Brownley Hill 494

A686

Sleeper Bridge

Gateposts

White Hill

R. West Allen

Long Cross

Clargillhead

Hartleycleugh

NORTHUMBERLAND

South View

CUMBRIA

**N**

**Gradient**

500
450
400
350
300
250
200
150
100
50
0

Metres above sea level

0     5     10     15     20     25     30     35     40 km

**Scale**

Km     1     2     3

Miles     1

## 28 Long Cross

| | |
|---|---|
| **Grade** | 21 Expert |
| **36.7 km** | **(22.8 Miles)** |
| **25.91 km** | Tarmac |
| **0.47 km** | Forest Road |
| **0.59 km** | Farm/Estate Road |
| **9.74 km** | Moorland Track/Path |
| **High Points:** | Brownley Hill 494m, Long Cross 482m, Keenleyside Hill 388m |
| **Maps:** | Ordnance Survey, Landranger 87 Hexham & Haltwhistle; Explorers OL43 Hadrian's Wall, & less than 4 km on OL31 North Pennines |
| **Facilities:** | Allendale Town – Tea Rooms, Pub Grub. Ninebanks YHA 87/771513$\frac{1}{2}$ |

### PLOTTING PLAN

| *START:* | Approach | Map Reference | Depart |
|---|---|---|---|
| Allendale Town | – | 837558 | WNW |
| Broadwood Halls Junction | E | 830$\frac{1}{2}$555 | SW |
| Flue Track | E | 817551$\frac{1}{2}$ | SW |
| BROWNLEY HILL | N | 796512 | S |
| South View Junction | N | 805$\frac{1}{2}$485 | NW |
| Bridge | N | 781$\frac{1}{2}$523 | NW |
| LONG CROSS | NE | 745501 | SW |
| Clargillhead | NE | 736498 | NNW |
| Old Road | SW | 747$\frac{1}{2}$520 | NE |
| Parmentley Road End | SSW | 776552 | SSE |
| Keenleyside Hill Foot | NW | 783538 | NE |
| KEENLEYSIDE HILL | WSW | 795548$\frac{1}{2}$ | ENE |
| Flue Track | NW | 817551$\frac{1}{2}$ | E |
| *FINISH:* | | | |
| Allendale Town | WNW | 837558 | – |

## Route Description

This is a route of slow speed toil and high speed reward. It goes either up or down. The nearest thing to flat is Allendale Town square. There is a lot of tarmac, but no apologies, There are three major climbs and an equal number of dashing descents. You will enjoy it. The countryside is bleak and beautiful with little cover – so go prepared – and the views are terrific. From the summit of White Hill you can see the Cheviots in the north, Cross Fell much nearer to the south, east to Tyneside and a long way west towards the Lakes. I will be honest. When doing the 'official' route assessment, John Carling and I encountered such weather we abandoned halfway around and went back the next day to finish it. We will quite gladly testify that if there is a westerly or south-westerly wind of any force, the climb up the Flue Track to the chimneys is hell. The steeper and rougher track up the east side of White Hill the next day was pure pleasure in comparison. The best recommendation for the loop is the fact that, despite all of this, John, on his first proper mountain biking route, bought the Bromwich he was riding when we got home. In fact we haggled and settled the deal at Keenleyside Hill Foot, and then he blew me off on the climb.

## Allendale Town to West Allendale

Depart from the Market Place down past the Hare and Hounds. Cross the bridge over the River East Allen and TL at the first opportunity at Gate House. TR steeply uphill after 130 metres. TL at the main road at the next junction then TR again at the first chance, again uphill and you are into it. It is usually about here that I stop to shed a layer of clothing! TL at the farm at the top of the hill onto a little road which becomes a track. Follow the flue all the way to the ridge. You can now see the chimneys, all you have to do is ride up there.

The chimneys and the Carriers Way we are following are all linked to the lead industry. In the early nineteenth century this was a major industrial area. Records show that in 1825 the Allen Smelt Mill (about 1 km downstream from the bridge we crossed after leaving the Market

Place) had two roasting furnaces, five ore hearths, two refining furnaces and one reducing furnace. Two chimneys were constructed to carry off the soot and smoke which was seriously detrimental to the health of the workmen and the surrounding vegetation down in the valley, and the Carriers Way is one of several in the district. These were packhorse routes from the various mines to the smelter. Strings of twenty-five 'galloways' would carry ore in sacks across the moors invariably led by a 'raker' – a horse that could be relied upon to choose the correct route. All of the animals would be muzzled to stop them eating tainted grass or drinking poisoned water – serious industrial pollution; but look at the countryside now. There are a couple of places where you can look inside the flue. Consider how clean it is. The reason for the cleanliness is commercial. Soot from the mill contained a high proportion of silver so, from time to time the flues were swept producing an annual income of between six and ten thousand pounds which was a lot of money in 1860.

Beyond the top chimney the track becomes less distinct and a greater challenge. Good technique here can save a lot of energy. Aim for the gate in the fence at the tarmac road. TR with the tarmac, around to Brownley Hill then down to South View junction. You can gauge how fast you are going when you cross the cattle grid halfway down. Is it a rattle, a brrrr, or a high pitched zip? TR at South View, SP Limestone Brae, which will again give you a clue to the industrial past. You will also find the name above the door of a gaudy chapel that was originally a Quaker Meeting House 2km down the road, and which now has a Buddhist Monastery next door. We turn hairpin L to cross the River West Allen at Ninebanks Church, but it is not always easy to see it when the trees are in leaf. Watch out for the SP for Mohope and Alston.

### West Allen Dale to Long Cross
TR across the bridge and follow a very pleasant road towards Mohope. Alas the good nature of the lane is short-lived. Just beyond the next junction it rears up the hill in a most alarming fashion. Continue straight past the road to the YHA onto the loose. Even the farmer's tractor misses

this bit, choosing an alternative route across the field, but it improves beyond the first gate. Zigzag to achieve the best line but beware the pools in the stream in the middle – some are quite deep. Beyond the sheep pens near the summit the track veers R and between two gateposts. No fence, no gate, just two gateposts. Then there is an entertaining stretch down to the Sleeper Bridge which has superseded Sandy Ford at Sandyford Sike. The far side looks tough, and it is. Get into a low gear, do not stand up, keep a grip, and you should make it. The final 400 metres over to Long Cross and the Cumbrian boundary has been resurfaced with tarmac 'shavings'.

## Long Cross to Allendale Town

A whizz through the forestry takes you to Clargillhead, then XRTR onto the A686 and back into Northumberland at Willyshaw Rigg. Go SO at the first corner in Northumberland onto the old road, a great piece of mountain biking. The thoroughfare is now grass-covered but much of it has a very firm base and you may see places where the moles have made little furrows across the top because it is impossible to burrow underneath. However, the first challenge lies only a short way in. Standing water fills the ruts, even in summer. Great sport. Try not to fall in. Follow the obvious road all the way back to the A686, just over 4 km.

Pause at the junction when you rejoin the tarmac and look across the valley. A stand of trees that was planted in the coronation year of George VI has the huge letters GR VI engraved, and from autumn through to spring can be easily seen. TL onto the A686 then TR off it at the next junction at Parmentley road end. SP Limestone Brae again, and follow to Keenleyside Hill Foot where we TL again for Allendale. This is one of the toughest bits of tarmac in England, or is it just that I invariably hit it late in the day? The higher you climb the easier it becomes, honest! Beyond Hawksteel Farm TR to return to the flue and retrace to Allendale Town. Finish off by enjoying the downhills.

***Long Cross.*** *Jubilation at the chimneys above Dryburn Moor, Long Cross still some distance away. In winter conditions consider dividing the route into two loops.*

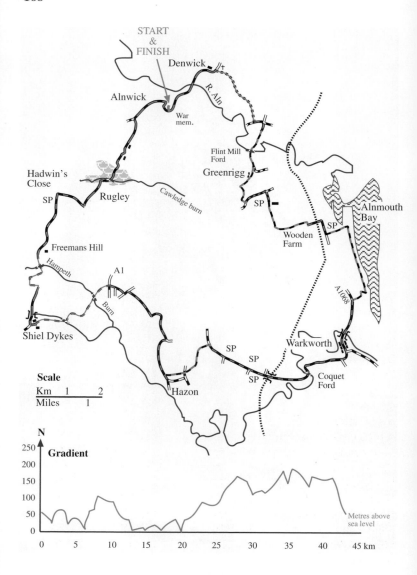

START
&
FINISH

Denwick

Alnwick

R. Aln

War
mem.

Flint Mill
Ford

Greenrigg

Hadwin's
Close

SP

Rugley

Cawledge burn

Alnmouth
Bay

Freemans Hill

Hampeth

A1

SP

Wooden
Farm

SP

Burn

A 1068

Shiel Dykes

SP

Warkworth

SP

SP

SP

Coquet
Ford

Hazon

**Scale**

| Km | 1 | 2 |
|----|---|---|
| Miles | 1 | |

**N**

250

**Gradient**

200

150

100

50

Metres above
sea level

0      5      10      15      20      25      30      35      40      45 km

# 29 Alnwick – Coast & Country

| | |
|---|---|
| **Grade** | 16 Energetic |
| **42.94 km** | **(26.68 Miles)** |
| **26.74 km** | Tarmac |
| **14.91 km** | Farm/Estate Road |
| **1.29 km** | Field/Dune Path |
| **High Point:** | Freemans Hill 192m |
| **Low Point:** | Alnmouth Bay Sea Level |
| **Maps:** | Ordnance Survey, Landranger 81 Alnwick & Morpeth; Explorer 332 Alnwick & Amble |
| **Facilities:** | Accommodation of every type available in Alnwick, the county town of Northumberland. Details available from Tourist Information Office, The Shambles, Alnwick, NE66 1TN. Accommodation, cafe, shops also in Warkworth |

## PLOTTING PLAN

| *START:* | Approach | Map Reference | Depart |
|---|---|---|---|
| Hotspur Carpark, Alnwick | – | 189132$^1/_2$ | SW |
| Hotspur Tower | NE | 188$^1/_2$132 | SE |
| War Memorial | NW | 190$^1/_2$131 | ENE |
| Denwick | W | 204$^1/_2$142$^1/_2$ | E |
| Flint Mill Ford | N | 216$^1/_2$118 | S |
| | NW | 214$^1/_2$101$^1/_2$ | NE |
| A1068 | WSW | 239097 | S |
| Alnmouth Box | W | 247095$^1/_2$ | S |
| A1068 Golf Course Road | ENE | 249072 | S |
| Morwick Road, Warkworth | NE | 240$^1/_2$052$^1/_2$ | NNW |
| Coquet Ford | NNW | 235$^1/_2$049$^1/_2$ | SSW |
| Disused Railway | SE | 206$^1/_2$055$^1/_2$ | WSW |
| Hazon | ENE | 192$^1/_2$045 | NW |
| Hampeth Crossroads | SE | 179072$^1/_2$ | NW |
| Field Road | NE | 173075 | SW |
| Shield Dykes | E | 150061$^1/_2$ | N |

| | Approach | Map Reference | Depart |
|---|---|---|---|
| Freemans Hill | SSW | 153086 | NNE |
| Hadwin's Close | SSW | 157$^1$/$_2$103 | E |
| Cawledge Burn Ford | W | 172$^1$/$_2$108$^1$/$_2$ | E |
| B6341, Clayport Bank | SSE | 180127$^1$/$_2$ | NE |
| Hotspur Tower | WNW | 188$^1$/$_2$132 | NE |
| *FINISH:* | | | |
| Carpark | SW | 189132$^1$/$_2$ | – |

## Route Description

This route was inspired by some of my favourite stretches of off-road riding, inevitably linked together by many bits of tarmac. It might appear very 'manufactured' but offers an enormous selection of terrain within the categories outlined in the route specification. It also provides interest and great views at any time of year. I would suggest summer time or at least a very dry spell, as the best time to undertake the tour. The first unbridged river crossing, Flint Mill Ford, boasts the most hazardous set of stepping-stones in the county and a ford with a very dubious bottom. If it is a beautiful, warm, sunny day try and ride it. I wish you luck. Otherwise wade across. Whatever you do, do not use the stepping-stones – you will set your neck. There are six fords of varying severity. All except two have optional bridges. If any are in spate do not attempt them. Getting drowned could spoil your day!

## Alnwick to The Coast

The carpark between the main street, Bondgate Without, and the Castle Walls NE of the Hotspur Tower is the Start and Finish point. Make your way back to the main street, TL along to the War Memorial, TL again onto the B1340 towards Bamburgh and you are on your way. This road skirts the parks of Alnwick Castle and it is well worth pausing after crossing the River Aln and looking back. There is a great view of the castle that you may well recognise from films or the Blackadder series. In Denwick village TR on the apex of the bend. Follow the tarmac up past the cottages and wait for the surface to deteriorate. This path is known locally as Rabbity Lonnen – watch out for the little conies – but the pheasants normally constitute a greater hazard when they run across your path. On reaching the main road, A1068, TL up the hill then R at the XR just over the brow. This takes you down to the notorious stepping-stones at Flint Mill Ford on the River Aln. There is no bridge alternative so, if the river is in spate, you must retrace to the XR and divert via Lesbury and Alnmouth Station. But this will not happen very often, and if the sun is shining and it is a beautiful summer's day it is not a bad place to abandon mountain biking and continue the route at a later date.

One day in early March, I was gingerly wading across, barefoot and frozen when I was suddenly aware of considerable noise to my left. In one movement I managed to secure a stable stance, reinforce my hold on my bike and look downstream, to see the biggest swan in the world coming in to land in the broken water on the other side of the stepping stones. He landed, shuffled his feathers into perfect order in two seconds, glanced across at me disdainfully whilst allowing himself to be carried down towards his mate who was selecting the choicest bits of weed from a section close to the bank, then completely forgot I was there. I formed the opinion that he just did it to alarm me.

At Greenrigg TR and follow the road past the buildings. This soon becomes a grassy track, then executes a 90°L turn uphill between two hedges. It demands a fair bit of technique to ride up to the gate. Then it is a case of jinking L and R through the whin bushes and following the track across the meadow. Check the O.S. map to see the shape of the track, which turns L up a hollow at the far fence. Even if you are not out of breath, pause and look back again as you close the gate, at another extensive view. TL onto the B1338 towards Alnmouth Station and follow this road 0.85 km to the farm road that leads to Bilton Barns. A SP confirms that you are in the right place. TR at the XR and follow the tarmac along to the farm. Just beyond the farm you could be forgiven for thinking that you have run out of road. The bridleway goes straight ahead hard against the eastern side of the fence. It is 390 metres of walking through deep grass. At the far side of the field, TL towards Wooden

Farm on a direct line between the Radio Mast and the buildings. Initially keep to the N side of the fence. After about 100 metres cross it to gain access to the farm track on the far side of the hedge. The track varies in route from time to time depending on the current crop – simply follow the tractor tracks which will become more pronounced as you near the farm. The track ends up in the farmyard. TR at the first opportunity and make your way down to the level crossing.

At the A1068, TR for 0.47 km then TL onto a stony bridleway signposted Buston Links. Stick to the obvious road all the way to and through the carpark area. **On leaving the carpark do not try to ride between the little posts – they have wire strung between them that can be obscured by grass in high summer.** Follow the obvious track along the dunes and up onto the heights above the bay. Below you is one of the finest beaches in Northumberland – clean, beautifully textured and usually very quiet. Have an apple at least or succumb to yet another temptation to forget about cycling for the day. The track drops down to a wooden bridge, then follow the road through the caravan park, across the golf course (another reason for wearing a crash helmet) and out to the A1068 again. TL and follow the main road to Warkworth Bridge, 1 km distant. A new section of the 'Costal Path' should be completed in 2005 which will eliminate the awkward stretch of A1068. Look for signs at the southern end of the caravan site, then stick to the coast. This will bring you out at Warkworth Bridge. Have a look at the old bridge and imagine lorries and vans negotiating it. I must confess to an error of judgement many years ago at this very spot. It required judicious use of the black enamel before the boss saw the side of the van.

Use the main street through the village. Apart from the obvious charm it is a great way to approach the castle at the top of the hill. Go SO past the castle entrance and follow the SP for Acklington. Then, in 0.9 km TR into Watersheugh Road and after that you cannot go wrong. Pass through Headier Lazes and continue WSW then SE to the ford at the River Coquet. This ford has a good concrete bottom. Keep to the middle. If there is a lot of water, use the footbridge upstream. TR with the tarmac and follow this road for a total of 3.15 km, turning L onto the old railway track 0.38 km beyond the Bank House junction. Rubble has been tipped at the end of the track but should prove no impediment to the mountain biker. This is yellowhammer country and you are likely to see several pairs at any time of the year. When you reach the tarmac again treat it as an offset junction. TL and immediately R for Hazon. At Hazon TJTR and N to Hazon High Houses, then N again to join a more main road near Southmoor. We now TL and head NW through another offset XR at Hampeth and across to the A1 Great North Road. Take care crossing the A1 to the field gate dead opposite. This gives access to over 3 km of good off-road track. After the second gate there is a mini-ford AND a little bridge – but you are not going to use that are you? Keep close to the fence on the L, then TR with the track along a line of well-weathered trees. Immediately after another gate we TL, keeping close to the fence again on the L. Soon after, the second ford presents itself. Again there is a soft option bridge, but the ford does require a fair amount of determination. In fact, in wet weather you could be forgiven for dodging it. I was once in a rally car that drowned out here!

Continue to follow the track to Shield Dykes farm. TJTR out of the farmyard and head N. Initially, there is 1 km of old tarmac, then follow the field road as it diverts to avoid the quarry which has eaten the old road. Consult the OS map and head for Freemans Hill. The road down to Hampeth Burn varies enormously with the weather conditions, so be prepared for a bit of slithering about, and a reasonably stiff climb on the far side. Join the tarmac again at Freemans Hill and head N to Hadwin's Close (158103) where it is XRTR. Just less than 1 km farther on we TL at a little XR. The SP has been broken for years, but it should say Rugley and Alnwick. Although tarmac, this is an enjoyable and testing bit of road, which includes the last ford through Cawledge Burn and brings you out at the top of Clayport Bank. You can freewheel down into Alnwick from here.

***Alnwick - Coast & Country.*** *Flint Mill Ford. River Aln. Any deeper than this, use the diversion. You may not have completed an RAF survival course!*

***Hexhamshire Common.*** *Winter morning, Hexhamshire Common. A privilege to be there.*

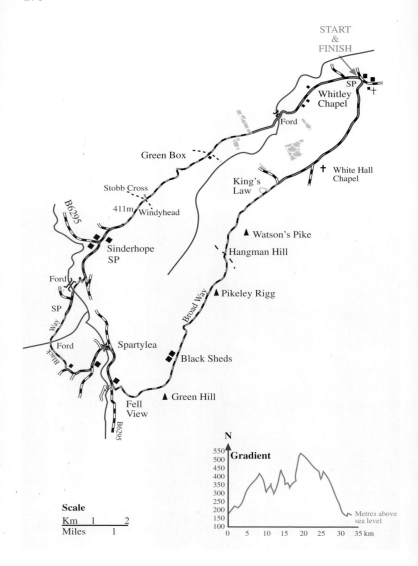

START & FINISH

SP

Whitley Chapel

Ford

Green Box

White Hall Chapel

King's Law

Stobb Cross

411m Windyhead

B6295

Watson's Pike

Sinderhope SP

Hangman Hill

Ford

SP

Broad Way

Pikeley Rigg

Black Way

Ford

Spartylea

Black Sheds

Fell View

Green Hill

B6295

**N**

**Scale**

Km    1    2
Miles    1

**Gradient**

550
500
450
400
350
300
250
200
150
100

Metres above sea level

0    5    10    15    20    25    30    35 km

# 30 Hexhamshire Common

| | |
|---|---|
| **Grade** | 19 Strenuous |
| **32.77 km** | **(20.36 Miles)** |
| **16.98 km** | Moorland Track/Path |
| **1.44 km** | Farm Road |
| **14.35 km** | Tarmac |
| **High Points:** | Windyhead 411m, Black Way 435m, Green Hill 529m |
| **Maps:** | Ordnance Survey, Landranger 87 Hexham; Explorer 31 North Pennines, OL43 Hadrian's Wall |
| **Facilities:** | None on route |

## PLOTTING PLAN

| *START:* | Approach | Map Reference | Depart |
|---|---|---|---|
| Whitley Chapel Crossroads | – | 87/927$^1$/$_2$577$^1$/$_2$ | W |
| Green Box | NE | 881553$^1$/$_2$ | SW |
| Windyhead | NE | 858$^1$/$_2$535 | SSW |
| B6295 | NE | 845520 | SW |
| Knockburn Ford | NE | 841509 | SW |
| Black Way | NNE | 834$^1$/$_2$490 | SSE |
| Spartylea Chapel | W | 850$^1$/$_2$489$^1$/$_2$ | SSE |
| Fell View | N | 852477$^1$/$_2$ | ESE |
| Green Hill | WSW | 865477 | ENE |
| Pikeley Rigg | SW | 884511 | NE |
| Kingslaw Plantation | SW | 902$^1$/$_2$543 | NE |
| *FINISH:* | | | |
| Whitley Chapel Crossroads | S | 927$^1$/$_2$577$^1$/$_2$ | – |

## Route Description

Hexhamshire Common is criss-crossed by a superb network of ancient bridleways and packhorse routes; a legacy from the days when these valleys and hills were the major lead mining area of England. It is hard to imagine industrial pollution of the worst kind affecting the whole of this region, but it did; and still does in one or two places. The land has obviously recovered to a large degree, a fact that should give hope to us all in these days of nothing short of environmental panic. But this is still a fairly frail environment that man can affect quite drastically in his passing. Tread as softly as you can. Of all the routes from 'The Shire' described in this guide, this is the toughest and the best. It is probably the easiest navigationally too, because it heads SW from Whitley Chapel straight across the Common to Sinderhope, then a bit more SW to Swin Hope only to cross the main Allen Dale road at Spartylea and head back along the magnificent Broad Way in a north-easterly direction. Weather conditions both prior to your trip and on the day can greatly affect the route and the amount of effort required. Make no mistake; this is a bleak and desolate tour in bad weather, to the point where you might be better advised to amend your plans and go somewhere else if the weather dictates.

### Whitley Chapel to Spartylea

Parking is limited at Whitley Chapel, but you can always ride the short distance to the 'Start'. Depart from the XR in a westerly direction towards Dalton, but at the very next junction go SO past the board declaring 'NO THROUGH ROAD FOR MOTOR VEHICLES'. You cannot refuse an invitation like that! The tarmac continues for another 2.6 km ending at a ford on the Rowley Burn. If you were a motorist you might say that the road deteriorated after that, but from a mountain biker's point of view, it improves considerably. Initially there is a steep broken climb which gives way to a gentler farm road. Then beyond the gate at Burntridge Plantation it 'improves' again and you are presented with a clarty track which soon becomes a mere sheep-track over the moor. Keep quite close to the wall on the L and you cannot go wrong. Eventually you will reach the Green Box. Go SO again following the wall for the next section to Stobb Cross. Then climb over the high point to Windyhead, 411m, before dropping down to Windyhead Gate on the edge of the moor. The moor in the area of Stobb Cross was devastated a couple of years ago by controlled burning which got out of hand. Please stick to the track and assist the keepers who are earnestly trying to encourage the growth of new heather.

A genuine 40 mph (or more!) decent follows the Hollocks Burn down to Sinderhope. TL onto the B6295 in the direction of Allenheads then TR after 1.38 km for another hurtle down to Knockburn Ford. Take care at the ford. Heed the depth posts. Use the bridge if in any doubt. The River East Allen can rise very quickly. Getting drowned could spoil your day! Continue SW from the ford onto the Black Way. Beyond the gate the track is rideable if the ground is dry and you are fit. Otherwise it is a walk for most of the way up the fellside to the tractor track where we TL and soon commence the drop to Swin Hope.

In this part of the Dale you will see many old buildings set in enclosures. These are the remnants of the old days when the inhabitants gleaned a living from two sources. Principally they were lead miners, but supplemented their income on small holdings with a few sheep, hens and perhaps a cow. Many of the houses have been modernised, but the permanent occupants still need the multi-source income approach. TL when you reach the tarmac at Swin Hope. Go L again at the bottom of the hill, and L yet again at the TJ at the old Board School. More downhill takes you to the bridge and the short climb to the main road at Spartylea Chapel.

### Spartylea to Whitley Chapel

Turn R (S) with the B6295 for 1.3 km to Fell View where we TL up the Fellside at a SP which says 'Hexhamshire'. There are posts bearing blue bridleway arrows to guide you up the hillside and if you can ride up here, you are good! Alex and I were plodding (well actually slipping and skidding) our way up here on foot one day in January when the cry drifted back, "There's ice up here, at least it's solid". And with that Alex got on his bike and rode away. It is a good place to stop and admire the view; look where you have been on the opposite side of the valley; look across to Killhope Law on the far ridge; speculate on routes that would take you into Durham or Cumbria, anything to ease the pain of this hill. But there is gain too. Eventually you hit the grouse road at the top of Byerhope Bank, then over the top of Green Hill, 529m, and you are away on the Broad Way, some of the best biking in Northumberland. Just over the top of Green Hill the bridleway cuts off a corner of the grouse road on a lesser, but still substantial, Landrover track. Less than 500 metres farther on we rejoin the 'main road'. Go past the black shooter's shed and head N on a new stretch of sandstone track. Alas, after 1.5 km the new road ceases at a gate – 'Route Degrade'.

Again it is a matter of opinion whether our route degrades? No, it becomes a major challenge. Usually wet, it provides everything a moor can throw at you, and it goes on and on. There is a brief respite after the gate at Pikeley Rigg. It is all uphill and loose. Then after you jink through the gate to cut across to Hangman Hill there is quite a test to get down to, and cross, the valley floor. At the gate take a line 45 degrees away from the fence. Keep on the lip of the little valley, and this will lead you down onto a track that the keepers have tried to establish, but it keeps sinking into the peat. Stay with it and it will guide you straight up to the 'XR' with the grouse road on Hangman Hill. XR SO at a little pile of stones. You will probably see the grouse road first, then realise that the rabbit track rising up the hill is ours. It is hard work but entertaining. Then there is my favourite downhill – technical, bumpy, a couple of ditches, and it goes on and on. I usually arrive at Kingslaw Plantation in a state of combined elation and distress. It is great. And there is the final tarmac downhill to Whitley Chapel, so button up your coat and go for it.

*Right: Cross Border Route. Looking NNE from the route through Newcastleton Forest. If you use a bit of imagination you can just make out the Bloody Bush Toll pillar on the skyline where the forest and moor meet.*

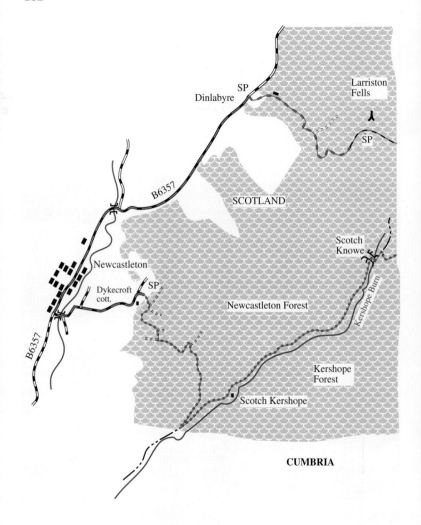

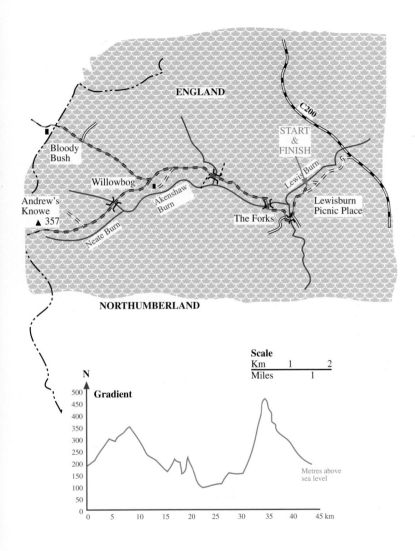

ENGLAND

C200

START & FINISH

Bloody Bush

Willowbog

Lewis Burn

Andrew's Knowe
▲ 357

Akenshaw Burn

Lewisburn Picnic Place

The Forks

Neate Burn

NORTHUMBERLAND

**Scale**

Km 1 2
Miles 1

N

**Gradient**

500
450
400
350
300
250
200
150
100
50
0

0 5 10 15 20 25 30 35 40 45 km

Metres above sea level

## 31 Cross Border Route

| | |
|---|---|
| **Grade** | 18 Strenuous |
| **43.09 km** | **(26.78 Miles)** |
| **1.24 km** | Moorland Track/Path |
| **3.35 km** | Forest Track/Path |
| **0.35 km** | Farm Road |
| **28.24 km** | Forest Road |
| **9.91 km** | Tarmac |
| **High Points:** | Andrew's Knowe 357m, Larriston Fells 467m |
| **Maps:** | Ordnance Survey, Landrangers 80 Cheviot Hills & Kielder Water, 79 Hawick & Eskdale; Explorer OL42 Kielder Water |
| **Facilities:** | Toilets at Lewisburn (except in winter). Pubs, grub and shops in Newcastleton. From October 2005 "The Rush" bike shack at Dykecrofts seven days a week in Summer. Food, bike hire, some spares. |

## PLOTTING PLAN

| *START:* | Approach | Map Reference | Depart |
|---|---|---|---|
| Lewisburn Picnic Place | – | 80/636896 | SW |
| Akenshawburn Bridge | ESE | 611$^1$/$_2$897$^1$/$_2$ | WNW |
| Willowbog Turnoff | ENE | 596897$^1$/$_2$ | SW |
| Andrew's Knowe | E | 568885 | W |
| Kershope Burn Bridge | NE | 560$^1$/$_2$883 | SSW |
| Kaim Brae | E | 79/549866$^1$/$_2$ | W |
| Scotch Kershope | NE | 524852 | SW |
| Gill | NE | 514846 | NNE |
| Forest Edge | SE | 503866 | N |
| Dykecrofts Cottage | E | 501$^1$/$_2$874 | SW |
| NEWCASTLETON | ESE | 480870 | NNE |
| Dinlabyre | SW | 529921 | E |
| Bloody Bush | WNW | 80/571910 | ESE |
| Akenshawburn Bridge | WNW | 611$^1$/$_2$897$^1$/$_2$ | ESE |
| *FINISH:* | | | |
| Lewisbum Picnic Place | SW | 636896 | – |

## Route Description

Cross Border Trail is the title given to a variation of this loop by the Forestry Commission and is signposted as such all the way. A tremendous bit of vision by the Commission has seen the development of this route linking related forests on both sides of the Border for the first time. What is even more remarkable is the fact that the new track over Andrew's Knowe has been specifically dedicated to bikes and horses. It is not wide enough for a vehicle. True to their word the FC completed their route, which is now marked on the OL42 as 'Cross Border Trail'. The link between Dykecroft Cottage and Larriston Fell is now finished, so you can shorten the ride a little, but you will miss out the visit to Newcastleton and the chance of food.

## Lewisburn to Kershope Burn

There are two ways to approach this route. Either use it as an extended training run and hammer it all the way, or take the whole day and enjoy the changes in countryside and terrain. There is ample parking at the Lewisburn Picnic Place. Depart SW on the main forest road. Follow it around past The Forks and gently warm to the task as you follow the Akenshaw Burn up towards Willowbog. The first 3 km are fairly flat; enough to get you mobile before the climbing starts beyond Akenshawburn bridge. There is a barrier just beyond the old turning down to Willowbog that is usually open. Then, 400 metres farther on we fork L onto a new forest road that takes us down to the Neate Burn, and we are on our way. Keep N of, and parallel to, the stream all the way up to the col on Andrew's Knowe, 357m. Do not be tempted to swing off R with the new road. Go SO onto the old sandstone track which you will find shrinks somewhat when you reach the new link section. You actually run downhill to the border at Scotch Knowe. Even before you enter Scotland, a board warning you that you are now entering Kershope Forest confronts you at the Cumbrian border. Within 200 metres you go from Northumberland into Cumbria then over the border into Scotland when you cross the Kershope Burn. This is currently the newest 'Border Bridge' and there is a great roller-coaster approach to it. If you succumb to temptation and go for maximum air time, you could well overshoot into the bracken. I did!

## Kershope Burn to Dinlabyre

Kielder Forest boasts some incredible names like Ding's Rigg, Binky Pike and Black Cuddy; but the Kershope and Newcastleton Forests caress the realm of the fantastic with Lazy Knowe, Queen o' Fairies Hole, The Caddrouns, Goose Rig, Short Shank, Swarf Moss, Muckle Punder Cleuch and Bessie's Bog. You have got to enjoy yourself in this company! Not only the names change (such as the English Cleugh becomes Cleuch) but this forest has a different feel. It is hard to identify, but the run down the road with the Kershope Burn, which upholds its role as the national boundary all the way to the Liddel Water at Kershopefoot, conveys a different ambience. Or is it just because it is downhill? Hug the water for more than 6 km until you see the board 'GILL' beyond Scotch Kershope. Here you TR up through a barrier and weave your way in company with the yellow marker all the way to the cattle grid above Dykescrofts Cottage. The totally off-road loop will eventually join up here, but for the time being we need a tarmac link, and perhaps a little refreshment in Newcastleton. TL over the grid, drop down to the cottage, TL again and whizz down to Newcastleton. Follow the B6357 N through the village and on to Dinlabyre where a faded, old, blue SP directs you up a 'Private Road' to Lewisburn.

## Dinlabyre to Lewisburn

Go straight over the top with only one, very minor navigational decision high up on the Larriston Fells – and even then there is a SP to show us the way to Bloody Bush. If only the riding was as easy as the navigation. We climb 344m (1129 feet) in 4.2 km (2.6 miles). The road is well-compacted, but its condition varies greatly with the volume of logging traffic it carries, and quite recently the weight of construction vehicles delivering the steelwork for the new transmitter at the top of the hill. Well that is my excuse – I will just have to get fitter and attack the brute with more determination. On a clear day the views are amazing

– more at every corner. But I got an even greater reward one winter day in freezing fog. Three roe deer seemed perplexed by my approach, one even wandering towards me. They were gorgeous and seemed reluctant to wander off, but deemed it more sensible to do so – quite a treat. You may even catch a rare sight of the elusive Cheviot goats on the crossing to Bloody Bush. So, apart from the achievement of climbing this monumental hill, there is wildlife galore, if you are quiet. The crossing to the toll pillar at Bloody Bush is reedy and wet in places, but technically entertaining. Then it is down, down and more down, 7.9 km to the Picnic Place to finish. Button up your coat and hammer it, even if you are just having a day out.

**188**

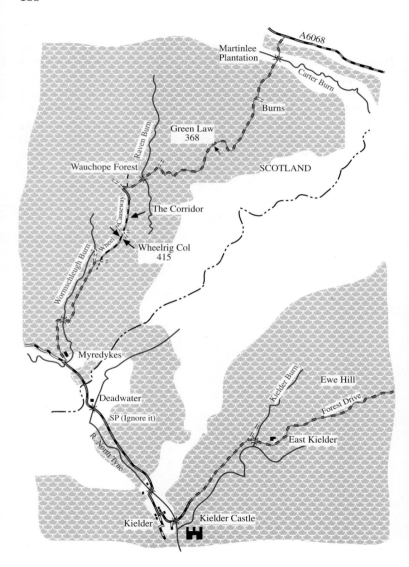

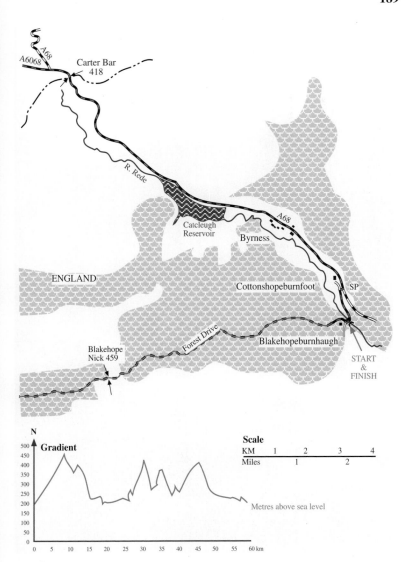

Carter Bar
418

A68

A6068

R. Rede

Catcleugh
Reservoir

Byrness

A68

ENGLAND

Cottonshopeburnfoot

SP

Forest Drive

Blakehopeburnhaugh

Blakehope
Nick 459

START
&
FINISH

N

**Gradient**

500
450
400
350
300
250
200
150
100
50

Metres above sea level

0   5   10   15   20   25   30   35   40   45   50   55   60 km

**Scale**

KM    1    2    3    4

Miles       1         2

***Wheel Causeway.*** *How to show a girl a good time. Wife Pam near Wheelrigg Head on a fresh , frosty morning. Honest, she always wanted to do the Wheel Causeway!*

## 32    Kielder Forest Drive & The Wheel Causeway

| | |
|---|---|
| **Grade** | 19 Strenuous |
| **58.24 km** | **(36.2 Miles)** |
| **28.13 km** | Tarmac |
| **27.97 km** | Forest Road |
| **2.14 km** | Forest Track/Path |
| **High Points:** | Blakehope Nick 459m, Wheelrig Col 415m, Green Law 368m, Carter Bar 418m |
| **Map:** | Ordnance Survey, Landranger 80 Cheviot Hills & Kielder Water; Explorers OL16 Cheviot Hills, OL42 Kielder Water |
| **Facilities:** | Caravan & Campsite at Byrness Forestry Commission, Youth Hostel in Byrness Village, Byrness Filling Station & Cafe open all year round, Byrness Hotel on A68, Picnic areas at Cottonshopeburnfoot and Blakehopeburnhaugh, and en route Bed & Breakfast at Cottonshopeburnfoot. Cafe at Kielder Castle in season |

### PLOTTING PLAN

| *START:* | Approach | Map Reference | Depart |
|---|---|---|---|
| Blakehopeburnhaugh | – | 784$^1$/$_2$002$^1$/$_2$ | W |
| Blakehope Nick | E | 712984 | WSW |
| Kielder Burn | E | 651959 | SW |
| Kielder | E | 626$^1$/$_2$935 | NNW |
| Myredykes | SE | 596981 | NE |
| Wormscleuch Burn | WNW | 596$^1$/$_2$992$^1$/$_2$ | NNE |
| Wheelrig Col | SW | 612018 | NNE |
| Wauchope Road | S | 613033 | E |
| Green Law | SW | 637$^1$/$_2$047 | E |
| Martinlee Plantation | SW | 656$^1$/$_2$080 | ESE |
| Carter Bar | NNW | 697$^1$/$_2$068 | SSE |
| Byrness Filling Station | NW | 771$^1$/$_2$022$^1$/$_2$ | SE |
| *FINISH:* | | | |
| Blakehopeburnhaugh | NE | 784$^1$/$_2$002$^1$/$_2$ | – |

## Route Description

The route breakdown shows about half the distance covered to be on tarmac. Frankly this surprised me, and has surprised many of my companions who have covered the circuit at various times of the year. Such is the severity of the terrain with four sustained climbs that there have been no complaints! The Wheel Causeway, an irresistible temptation for mountain bikers if there ever was one, is an ancient route of which little in reality remains. The earliest record of its existence is found in Edward I's journey of 1296, and it is reasonable to suppose that the 'old way of Roxburgh' which is mentioned in connection with a 12th century land grant at Kershope, some miles to the SW, followed a similar course. The route of the causeway is marked on the O.S. map from Deadwater Farm in a northerly direction. But accept my word for it, there is little or no trace on the ground and the route described here is the only rideable stretch – and you will need to walk some of this. The climb over Green Law can be a real grind in winter when the sun is low and the ground wet, and even the tarmac up onto the Carter Bar (another ancient trade route), can provide little in the way of relief. But all is forgiven on the high speed descent to Catcleugh, and the final approach to Byrness village late on a winter's afternoon has a charm all of its own. At that time of year even the A68 is virtually deserted, you are down off the tops in the shelter of the valley, and on a calm day the smoke plumes from every house in the village seem to signal all is well – you have made it.

## Start

The Start and Finish are located at Blakehopeburnhaugh which is reached from the A68 road by turning in at the SP for Cottonshopeburnsfoot, Kielder via the Forest Drive and then immediately L following the signs for the Forest Drive. (Fig. 21/1)

## Blakehopeburnhaugh to Kielder Castle

I am tempted to say that this bit is easy. You simply follow the Forest Drive all the way from Blakehopeburnhaugh to Kielder. But it is not, particularly if there is a wind from the W or SW. The route climbs some

255m to Blakehope Nick, 459m, in 8.3 km and can be a daunting task. One windy day I recall being so sick of the whole enterprise that I turned around at the top and came back, only to find myself sitting by the River Rede thirteen minutes later wondering why I had not gone on. Mind, the descent was worth it. Kielder Castle is situated 20.09 km across the Forest Drive. Route finding is easy – you simply follow the main 'road', which is usually in very good condition. There are Picnic Places at Blackblakehope, 3.1 km, White Crag, 4.6 km, Sandy's Gears, 11.31 km, and Kielder Burn, 15.5 km. But make no mistake, this can be a bleak track and the top five or six kilometres can be a bit wild at times.

Each year the tarmac spreads E from Kielder. At the time of writing it had almost reached East Kielder Farm but it in no way detracts from the enjoyment. In fact, if you have flown down from Ewe Hill your wrists

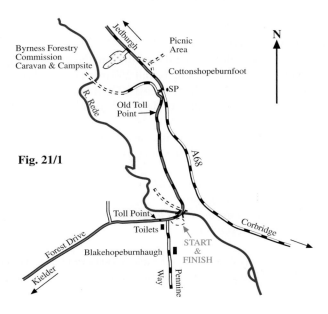

**Fig. 21/1**

and neck will appreciate the respite. Kielder Castle was built as a shooting box for the first Duke of Northumberland. Now an administrative centre for the Forestry Commission, it houses an interesting exhibition which gives an insight into the flora and fauna of the forest. It is worth a visit if you have the time. I have found that you see more animals, particularly deer, when riding a mountain bike than on foot. No doubt you come upon them quicker but you are much quieter too – no thumping boots. An extreme example of this took place on an extension of this route, on a northerly spur of the Wheel Causeway. Alex Spence was leading down a firebreak towards Hardlee – which sensible folk would have decided was unrideable – fighting over grassy tussocks, through sphagnum stoppers and downhill into a stiff breeze, when suddenly a white crash helmet peeled off right and a white rump shot off left. He had been within a metre of ramming a roe deer from behind before she heard him. I do not know who got the bigger fright, but I know who got the best laugh.

### Kielder Castle to Myredykes
Follow the SP for Kielder Water downhill from the castle and again, as you cross the bridge at the foot of the hill 250 metres later TR up through the village past the village shop. Then TJ TR at the 'main' road to take you up the top end of the valley of the North Tyne.

Many years ago the poet Swinburne extolled this locality in his 'Jacobite's Exile'. I feel that it has not changed much since.

*On Kielder-side the wind blaws wide,*
*There sounds nae hunting-horn*
*That rings sae sweet as the winds that beat*
*Round bank where Tyne is born.*

Stay with the tarmac across the border into Scotland and on to Myredykes. At Myredykes TR then second L up the hill to the gate in the wall. (Fig. 21/2)

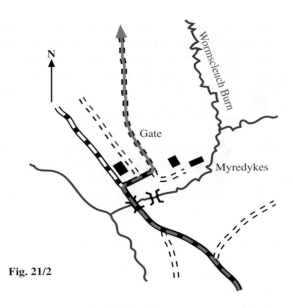

**Fig. 21/2**

## Myredykes to Martinlee Plantation

Crunch time. If in doubt go up. We cannot ride the Wheel Causeway
until we reach Wheelrigg Col but good forest roads run more or less
parallel to it and they are a substantial challenge in themselves. From
Myredykes take the high road N into the forest climbing steadily past a
road on the L. Then drop down to cross the Wormscleuch Burn.
Immediately across the burn TL steeply uphill parallel to, but 200 metres
W of the Wheel Causeway. TR at the second junction (at 1.97 km) just
before the road descends again. Then 270 metres further up the side
road, TL onto the Causeway itself. This is the hard bit.

All that remains at this point is an avenue through the trees that eventually
leads up to the col. Choose the best deer track and head on past the
ancient fenceposts. On reaching quite a wide, treeless area, 0.48 km
after leaving the forest road, go straight across aiming for the highest

their cattle through. In wet weather they also provide the best route for exit. A better defined track will then lead you to Wheelrig Col, 415m, at the ancient gateposts. Beyond the gateposes there are raised stances at either side of the track. This is were the drovers would stand and count riding, although they can be a trifle lumpy. A short way beyond the stances, two new forest roads intersect the Causeway in quick succession. But we go SO. About 40 metres beyond the second road, the route becomes rideable again and you follow your nose into 'The Corridor'. This is a damp downhill, paved with pine needles, grasses and sphagnums. The excitement is directly proportionate to your bravery. But sadly the trees are approaching maturity and in preparation for felling, a new forest road has been made which heralds the end of 'The Corridor' as we know it.

Join the new road, then 350 metres farther on, leave it again going SO at the first bend between the larches and pines. The last 180 metres take you to the main forest thoroughfare, the Wauchope Road. Being the main road this track varies in condition from time to time, but is usually very fast down to the Raven Burn. On one occasion when I considered it less than perfect I was scuttling down the hill at a fair rate only to be overtaken by Malcolm Williams and Paul Eynon, one either side, the latter shouting "forty-two" as they passed. It was mph not kph – a good descent. Of course all this enjoyment must be paid for. 1.2 km after joining this main road we TR at the Greencleuch junction and start the climb to Green Law, 368m. Up, up, and a bit more up. Still on the main road, it is perfectly rideable but sustained and steep. If it is a nice day I usually have my orange at the top. If it is not I wait until I have descended to Burns over 3 km further on. Beyond Burns the road climbs a little again, for the last time in the forest. Then it is down to the Carter Burn and up the last rough to Martinlee Plantation.

### Martinlee Plantation to Blakehopeburnhaugh

The instruction TJ TR should be a great relief as we join the A6088 and head towards the Carter Bar, 418 m, some 4.5 km distant. Initially it is, but then we start to climb again. Take your time. It is harder than it looks. You can pause on the top of the Carter Bar and take a photograph against the national boundary stone with the tourists – but I bet you have put more effort into your tour than any of them. In the summer there is usually a mobile tea shack and an ice cream van, but in winter there will only be the lorry drivers and you. Refreshment will have to wait until you reach the haven of the Byrness Filling Station. Even on a mountain bike you can beat some of the cars down into Redesdale. Then it is quietly along the side of Catcleugh Reservoir with its varied birdlife, and on to Byrness. Then you are back onto the toll road at Cottonshopeburnfoot and cycling down to the Finish at Blakehopeburnhaugh.

What did you see on the way? What did you find on the way? Was it a mini-achievement? Of course it was.

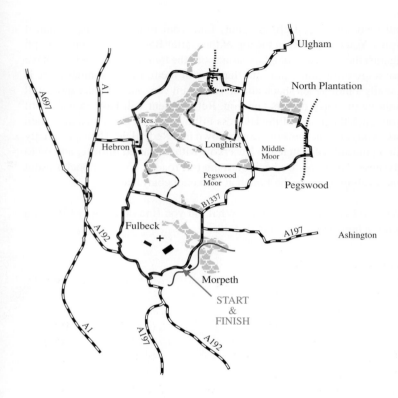

Ulgham

North Plantation

A697

A1

Res.

Hebron

Longhirst

Middle Moor

Pegswood Moor

Pegswood

B1337

Fulbeck

A197

Ashington

Morpeth

START
&
FINISH

A192

A1

A197

A192

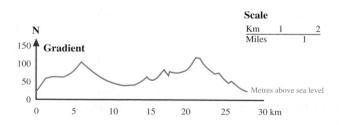

**Scale**

| Km | 1 | 2 |
|---|---|---|
| Miles | 1 | |

**N**

**Gradient**

150
100
50
0

Metres above sea level

0    5    10    15    20    25    30 km

## 33   Butterwell Bridleways

| | |
|---|---|
| **Grade** | 11 Sporting |
| **27.55 km** | **(17.12 miles)** |
| **0.78 km** | Field Path |
| **1.52 km** | Farm Track |
| **8.12 km** | Farm Road |
| **17.13 km** | Tarmac |
| **High Point:** | Hebron Reservoir 114m. |
| **Maps:** | Ordnance Survey Landranger 81 Alnwick & Morpeth, Explorer 325 Morpeth & Blyth. |
| **Facilities:** | Morpeth has all the facilities one would associate with a market town – except a mart! |

## PLOTTING PLAN

| *START:* | Approach | Map Reference | Depart |
|---|---|---|---|
| East Mill layby, A197, Morpeth | – | 203864$^1$/$_2$ | E |
| B1337 near Pegswood Moor | S | 211$^1$/$_2$879 | WNW |
| Near East Shield Farm | SE | 200885 | NNE |
| E of Hebron Reservoir | SW | 198902 | E |
| B1337 Longhirst village | W | 225891 | E |
| Longhirst Crossing | WSW | 240895 | N |
| North Plantation | S | 237905$^1$/$_2$ | W |
| Dukes Coverts, W of B1337 | E | 221906 | S |
| 'Workshops Junction' | SE | 208906 | NNE |
| Uncl. Rd W of The Cockles | S | 212$^1$/$_2$916 | W |
| Cockle Park | ENE | 200912 | WSW |
| Hebron | E | 196897 | S |
| Fulbeck | N | 191877 | S |
| Morpeth, Manchester Street | NW | 197861$^1$/$_2$ | E |
| *FINISH:* | | | |
| East Mill layby, Morpeth | WSW | 203864$^1$/$_2$ | - |

## Route Description

You won't find Butterwell on any current Ordnance Survey map, possibly because it disappeared under opencast coal mining operations many years ago, but now this area has been reinstated in the most pleasing fashion, not least in the provision of good tracks that have been given bridleway status, allowing some surprisingly good riding with great views of the surrounding countryside. I need to thank CTC's David Roberts for taking me around on a 'proving' ride, because not only do the current maps not have the bridleway graphics superimposed, several stretches of tracks aren't even shown! A departure from the strip-mining scenario is the straight-line bridleway between North Plantation and Duke's Coverts, something I have ignored for years because it didn't connect with anything else, but it adds an entertaining dimension and a bit of a test in the single-track section. Biggest surprise of the whole route is the wide tarmac section right in the middle through Blubbery Wood – better than the nearby A1!

## Morpeth to Longhirst

The 'START' layby at East Mill is just beyond the speed de-restriction signs on the N side of the A197, a bend of the old road immediately prior to the entrance to East Riding Clinic, but there are kerbs as you turn in. There is a new cycle track on the south side of the road which carries you E then NE up the Worral Bank alongside the A197. Follow this for 1.72 km to Pegswood road end, where A197 turns R but we go straight on with B1337 for another 0.39 km to the next bend where the route turns L towards Hebron. After a further 1.45 km turn R off the tarmac, just beyond the entrance to East Shield Farm, into a stony farm road up the side of the new golf course. There is a 'bridleway' fingerpost and a slot on the R of the galvanised gates for bikes. Ride NE initially, then swing L and L again until you are riding W when the stony road ceases after 0.79 km and the bridleway continues as a path alongside the crops to a wicket gate at the trees. Turn R at the gate for another (often wet) 200 metres to double gates where the route is confirmed by a blue bridleway arrow and a wide farm road takes you onwards past the wooden summer-house and roughly N past Hebron village. After 1.21 km you reach a 'T-junction' just E of Hebron Reservoir where the route turns R, downhill, but pause and admire the view out to the coast. The now familiar stony road heads roughly E for 2.98 km to Longhirst Dairy – which doesn't exist any more – but pools are frequent and there is a 'soft' stretch alongside the golf course which can be a bit of a test after rain. Look for the overgrown slot on the R immediately after double galvanised gates with barbed wire and jink R into the skinny path when the main track bears L at the end of the golf course. Follow your nose E for 0.58 km into Longhirst village, paying due respect to the little paved ford in the trees.

## Longhirst to Cockle Park

With due care cross B1337 in Longhirst and head E, SP 'Linton' past Middle Moor for 1.92 km to the T-junction just beyond Longhirst railway crossing. Turn L at the T-junction, SP 'Linton', then L again at the first corner after 200 metres SP 'Ulgham' – pronounced Uffam – back over the railway, R past the cattery and look for a white gate with a wooden Bridleway, Duke's Coverts fingerpost on the L after 1.35 km. Running WNW for 1.52 km the initial 3-ply bridleway shrinks to single track after 280 metres, dodges around a fallen tree and eventually becomes substantial field road prior to the B1337. On reaching the main road turn L for 200 metres towards Longhirst, then R through a gate back onto Butterwell farm roads at SP "Bridleway, Tritlington Road", then L again after another 110 metres opposite a discreet little post bearing the bridleway arrows and you're on your way. The road swings R and heads WNW through two gates that obviously double as part of the sheep pen complex, then gently uphill to a strange shaped XR on a crest. On the crest swing R along a stretch of farm road that always seems to be wet, aiming to pass to the R of the big grey shed – the old opencast workshops – then R again, at what is basically TJTR, after 330 metres onto exceptionally wide downhill tarmac through Blubbery Wood. Enjoy it. After 1.62 km when confronted by exceptionally wide locked gates at a workshops made 'Give Way' SP turn L onto the final wide dirt road.

Then ride parallel, but above the opencast 'highway' to the Tritlington road W of The Cockles. TJTL onto the public road, towards Tritlington, but there is no SP. Head W for 0.82 km then fork L over a crest, SP 'Hebron', and up through Cockle Park farm as you turn S to return to Morpeth.

## Cockle Park to Morpeth

It is now tarmac all the way to the Finish. Follow this country road over the E flank of Hebron Hill past Hebron Reservoir and flash down into Hebron itself. Then TJL, SP 'Morpeth', and down again for 1.24 km to the junction on the corner at West Shield Hill where, with care because the view is poor, we keep R into the singletrack road SP 'Morpeth'. This carries you down through Fulbeck, where the burn covers the road so frequently it could well be a 'dry' ford – with grit – into the sting in the tail in the shape of a nasty little hill. Then merge L onto the A192 at the top of Pottery Bank and down into Morpeth. Then TL at the first traffic lights in the town, at Appleby's Bookshop, on the corner of Manchester Street, after 3.16 km, then turn L at the Wellwood mini-roundabout after 120 metres, then XRTR into Howard Terrace after another 80 metres and E along to A197. TJTL at the end of Howard Terrace, SP "A197 Ashington" and down past the 30s to the layby. Total distance 27.55 km.

*Right: Butterwell Bridleways. Little now remains of the opencast operations, except the spare bucket for 'Big Geordie', the huge dragline that did most of the excavation. Local patter has it that if you carry it away, you can have it! My bike dwarfed.*

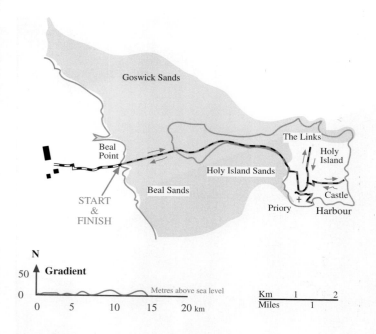

## PLOTTING PLAN

| START: | Approach | Map Reference | Depart |
|---|---|---|---|
| Beal Sands car park (mainland) | – | 75/080427 | ENE |
| Holy Island – to pass | | | |
| Lindisfarne Hotel | N | 126420½ | E |
| N end of Straight Lonnen | S | 129431 | S |
| Near Sheldrake Pool | WSW | 138423 | WSW |
| Harbour – Steel End | NNE | 129418½ | NNE |
| Chare Ends | ESE | 123426 | NNW |
| FINISH: | | | |
| Beal Sands car park | ENE | 080427 | – |

# 34    Lindisfarne or Holy Island

| | |
|---|---|
| **Grade** | 8 Sporting |
| **19.68 km** | **(12.23 miles)** approximately – you are sure to deviate once on the island! Any road on the island, especially the cause way, can and probably will have a coating of sand to a greater or lesser degree, so take any 'tarmac' mileage with a pinch of sea salt! |
| **7.27 km** | Rough Island Roads |
| **12.41 km** | Tarmac |
| **High Point:** | Chare Ends corner 15m! |
| **Maps:** | Ordnance Survey Landranger 75 Berwick-upon-Tweed, Explorer 340 Holy Island & Bamburgh. |
| **Facilities:** | Lindisfarne Hotel, Ship Inn and snacks from Holy Island Post Office. Occasionally, at the appropriate time of year, crab sandwiches from the fishermen's cottages en route to the castle. Summer café and ice cream vans. |

### Route Description

Undoubtedly the trip to Holy Island is not a 'mountain bike' route in the purest sense, but it is unusual, fun and packed with interest. The fun element might diminish somewhat in a strong westerly, which can make the return trip across the exposed causeway quite dire, and getting marooned in the refuge box may ruin your day completely. HEED THE TIDE TABLES displayed at the roadside outside Beal Sands car park. Automated advance information on crossing times is available 24 hrs. by telephoning Berwick-upon-Tweed Tourist Information Centre, 01289 330 733.

Lindisfarne or Holy Island was the core of Christianity in Northumbria. The successful prime movers were a group of Irish monks from Iona led first, in 643 AD by Aidan and later by Cuthbert, probably the favourite saint of Northumbria, affectionately commemorated to this day in the local name for the wild eider ducks, usually referred to as 'Cuddies' or 'Cuddy Ducks'. Only a true island for about six hours each day, safe crossing windows also usually last six hours too, but despite the tarmac base – completely renewed in 2004 – high spring tides regularly cover the road. You may find a seaweed strewn, sandy piste to follow.

The ride has two distinct sections, the long stint across the causeway and back, and a poach around the island. It is unlikely that you will be able to ride the full length of Straight Lonnen to the northern side of the island, or Crooked Lonnen to the east, due to windblown sand, but do your best without ruining your bearings!

If possible choose a bright winter day for your trip. There is nothing to stop you undertaking a summer tour, but there will be far fewer folk during the winter and lots more wildfowl. Obviously the number of seabirds you will see as you ride across the flats, known locally as The Swad, will depend when you go and the state of the tide, but many of the waders seem well used to the passage of traffic and will continue to feed close to the road as you pass. It's an excellent opportunity to see redshank, snipe, curlew, oyster catchers, swans, geese and the inevitable 'Cuddies' at close quarters. A major bonus is the fact that the population will change for the return journey due to the tide.

Riding along the main street and down to the harbour will open up a deal of interest not least of which is the row of old upturned boats used for gear storage by the fishermen. The only reminder of the old trade with the Continent, mainly cured herring to the Baltic states, is the Rabies Control notice on the harbour wall, but one can only speculate who might enforce any regulations when the tide is in, there being no permanent police or coastguard presence on the island.

Ride around the village, pedal slowly through the narrow streets and inevitably you will end up at the priory. Even if you are not ecclesiastically minded some of the gravestones are worth a read.

**Beal Sands (mainland) car park to Holy Island village.**
Navigation couldn't be easier. Simply follow the tarmac causeway ENE past the white refuge to the island, then hug the dunes as the road swings ESE. After 6.12 km turn first L, past the Lindisfarne Hotel, coach park, then L again up past St. Coombs farm and N on the bumpy track as far as you can ride, probably about the Lindisfarne Nature Reserve sign.

**Around the island.**
Retrace S back down Straight Lonnen to St. Coombs farm, then head E along Crooked Lonnen, if possible to the E coast. Once again you may be stopped by drifted sand. Ted Hall, frequent training partner and keen gardener, insists I draw your attention to the walled castle garden, map ref. 136419, between Crooked Lonnen and the Castle, originally created by the famous Gertrude Jekyll about 1912 and currently undergoing restoration! Back again to the village then weave your way around to the harbour. There is a seat among the lobster pots near the end of the pier that affords a grand view of the castle and all the goings on in the harbour. By the time we had wiggled our way back to the main junction we had recorded a further 7.45 km, so all that remains is the return journey along the causeway. The intermittent string of poles taking a more direct line between Chare Ends and Beal Sands is the course of the old crossing, now often called the Pilgrim's Route, much wetter and subject to shifting sands. As a child I recall roughly following the poles in what seemed to be a huge old pre-war car, and told to put my feet on the seat to prevent a soaking when the water came in – and it did. All very exciting, nearly as good as riding across on a bike! Total distance 19.68 km.

**Lindisfarne or Holy Island.** *All the brochures of Holy Island have a picture of the castle. You can't miss it, however, don't lose sight of the fact that this is still a working community, the harbour being the focus of most activities.*

*Graeme Purdy climbing the deceptively steep tarmac near Hetherington.*

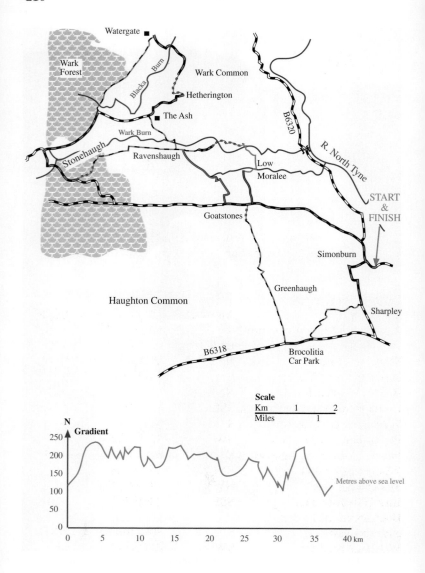

## 35    Watergate

| | |
|---|---|
| **Grade** | 20 Strenuous |
| **36.94 km** | **(22.95 miles)** |
| **3.16 km** | Grass & moorland. |
| **11.21 km** | 4WD & moorland track. |
| **1.90 km** | Forest & farm road. |
| **20.67 km** | Tarmac - mostly single-lane, often loose and muddy. |
| **High Point:** | Teppermoor Hill 233m. |
| **Maps:** | Ordnance Survey Landranger 87 Hexham & Haltwhistle, Explorer OL43 Hadrian's Wall. |
| **Facilities:** | Space for four cars in the 'Start' layby. Pubs/hotels in Wark at 860770, Chollerford at 919706, but excellent pub grub ( and restaurant if you wish to impress some one!) at 'The Hadrian' on A6079 in Wall village at 916688. |

### PLOTTING PLAN

| *START:* | Approach | Map Reference | Depart |
|---|---|---|---|
| Layby off B6320 Simonburn | – | 87/881733$\frac{1}{2}$ | NW |
| Hall Barns | ENE | 873$\frac{1}{2}$734 | SSE |
| Sharpley – bridleway | NNW | 877$\frac{1}{2}$723 | W |
| Teppermoor Hill, 233m | E | 867722 | S |
| B6318, Military Road | NNW | 864713 | WSW |
| Crook Burn, near Greenhaugh | SSE | 853721 | NNW |
| Ward Lane crossroads | S | 844$\frac{1}{2}$751 | W |
| Ravenshaugh T-junction | SW | 826$\frac{1}{2}$766 | W |
| Pennine Way, Longlee Rigg | E | 811767$\frac{1}{2}$ | SSW |
| Windy Edge wood | ENE | 801764$\frac{1}{2}$ | SW |
| Stonehaugh road | NW | 796$\frac{1}{2}$757$\frac{1}{2}$ | W |
| Birk Hill crossroads | SSE | 786$\frac{1}{2}$767 | ENE |
| Blackaburn road end – bridleway | S | 801776 | NNE |
| Watergate road end | SW | 817$\frac{1}{2}$799 | SE |

|                               | Approach | Map Reference | Depart |
|-------------------------------|----------|---------------|--------|
| Wark Common                   | NNE      | 824786        | SSW    |
| The Ash – old road            | NE       | 816½776       | SE     |
| Ravenshaugh (W)               | N        | 824767        | E      |
| Ramshaws Mill – old road      | WSW      | 843768        | S      |
| Low Moralee                   | N        | 847761½       | SW     |
| Ward Lane crossroads          | N        | 844½751       | E      |
| Townhead, B6320               | NW       | 877741        | S      |
| *FINISH:*                     |          |               |        |
| Simonburn layby               | NE       | 881733½       | –      |

## Route Description

You will see from the Plotting Plan that this is one for fit navigators. The route, through some seldom visited but quite dramatic Northumbrian countryside, includes a couple of old roads now seeing little use, some fine wild bridleways and even a tiny stone circle – the Goatstones – which isn't marked on the OS map. At the other end of the timescale we use one of the newest public roads in Northumberland – the sweeping stretch into Stonehaugh that started life as a Forestry road but was such a popular short cut with the locals it was eventually metalled. I must admit I enjoyed it more with an 'East African' dust plume behind me!

## Simonburn to Stonehaugh

Depart NW towards Wark on B6320, turn L into a single track road at trees before the bend and ride WSW to Hall Barns farm, reached in 0.63 km (0.39 mile). TJTL at the farm into a narrower single-track road through what once had been a gate and steeply uphill through a cutting past a Gates warning sign. Turn L and immediately R at the next strange-shaped junction onto an even lesser road that climbs to Sharpley. The next turn onto a field bridleway comes after a further 1.24 km. Fifty metres beyond the farm entrance turn R through a wooden gate onto the little-used bridleway, no SP. Initially keep close to the little wood on the L, then cut across bumpy ground to a wall and after 190 metres a bridleway sign on another gate confirms the route. Hug the wall all the way to the top of

Teppermoor Hill, reached after 1.11 km, the highest point on the route. It's another 1.06 km across to the Military Road at High Teppermoor so turn L through the gate, head S towards pines on the far hill, follow a well defined track to the farm, then SE out onto the main road.

Turn R, with care onto B6318, down past Brocolitia car park looking to turn R again at the bottom of the hill, SP Public Bridleway, Greenhaugh. The track is tarmac for only 20 metres, then rutted grass. Follow a straight line NNW for 1.80 km to the Crook Burn finally approached down a muddy hill. It is another 2.85 km before you strike the farm road at Goatstones. Continue NNW from the Crook Burn, past Greenhaugh, the castellated farmhouse on the hill, NNW again with the wall. Wiggle down through the ford at Hopeshield Burn. An element of 'and do what you think is best', which probably includes swinging sharp R across to a windswept tree, then following the wall NNW again, down through the rocky ford at the Castle Burn then up over the nose of Haggle Rigg. The bridleway then all but disappears, the wall becomes even less of a wall, so aim for the middle of the copse at the bottom of the hill beyond the power lines then swing L to Goatstones farm road.

The farm road up to Ward Lane at the top of the hill seems harder than it should be! Turn L at the XR towards Stonehaugh, then look to turn R into a narrower single-track road after 1.16 km. No SP but head N for 2.40 km on the near mountainous little road to Ravenshaugh. Turn L at Ravenshaugh TJ and head W for 1.63 km on an ever deteriorating (or improving, depending on your point of view) road to the Pennine Way. Don't cross anything, simply turn L down the E side of the wall for 110 metres, then R onto a reasonable moorland track. There are one or two tiny bridges, the going becomes steeper, rougher and wetter, but continue straight for the trees, reached after 0.72 km. Straight on into the forest, a bit of a test. The bridleway and the stone wall seem to have merged to create a very lumpy track, well defined but very lumpy just the same. Very difficult when wet for 340 metres to forest TJ where you turn L onto a very grassy track, easy to follow but hard to ride. When the bridleway turns to forest road, follow it over the brow and down to tarmac after 1.37 km. Turn R onto the tarmac which whizzes you down into Stonehaugh, through the village and along to Warksburn picnic place, a good place to dine al fresco at the totem poles.

## Warksburn to Simonburn

Ride NNW up the hill from the picnic place to the old school at Birk Hill XR where you turn R, no SP for us, and follow the wide undulating road E, then NE for 1.92 km to Blackaburn road end, where the tarmac turns sharp R. The ride route goes straight ahead through the field gate (NNE), slightly away from the wall on the L. Then through sheep pens, back across to the wall, across the Blacka Burn and NE for 3.19 km to the public road from Wark. Initially you follow the forest edge, then aim for a 'garden' gate through pasture keeping R of the fence but very close to it. When the Watergate farm road is reached keep R again to the TJ. You only follow this tarmac SE for 1.21 km – crossing the Blacka Burn again which swung N and followed you – before turning R (SSW) onto a steep tarmac uphill which doubles as the Pennine Way. After 1.38 km this brings you to a gated junction on the ridge at Hetherington.

Turn R through the gate onto a wider road past Hetherington - there is a SP saying 'Stonehaugh' if you go across and read it – then look for 'The Ash' farm after 1.34 km. There is no SP or apparent nameplate for the farm, just look for the ash trees. Turn L off the main road, follow the arrows that guide you S across the paddock as soon as you enter the farmyard, then down the side of the fields on an old grassy road. Check the Warks Burn ford before diving in, it is prone to flooding. You can of course opt for the bridge straight away. The climb at the far side can be rough, the total to Ravenshaugh (W) is 1.51 km – seems like a lot of action for the distance!

On reaching the Ravenshaugh road turn L, along your previous route for 220 metres then SO (E) past Longlee, across the Warks Burn, by bridge, and after 2.04 km turn steeply downhill to Ramshaws Mill, no SP, when the road swings L uphill. Ramshaws Mill is only named on the OS Explorer. Wiggle through modernised farm buildings then half R through an old gate into a leafy old road that climbs steeply uphill. Follow the line of trees out into open farmland then S to Low Moralee 0.95 km later. On reaching tarmac again turn R and ride W then S for 1.35 km on narrow, often muddy, up and down rural road to Ward Lane XR . The final flee is accessed by turning L at the XR, riding over a small summit 800 metres to the E, then down, down, down all the way to Townhead 3.59 km. All that remains is half a mile of B6320 roughly S to the layby, but the last bit is uphill. Sorry!

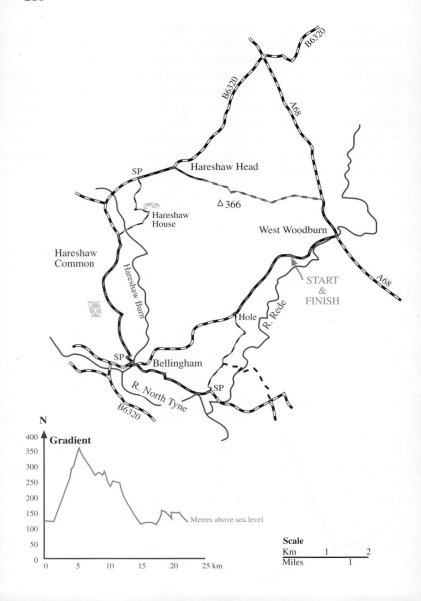

Km 1 2
Miles 1

Scale

## 36   Percy's Moss

| | |
|---|---|
| **Grade** | 18 Strenuous |
| **22.29 km** | **(13.85 miles)** |
| **0.85 km** | Moorland path |
| **2.22 km** | Farm track |
| **1.96 km** | Farm road |
| **17.26 km** | Tarmac – but be warned some of the tarmac is genuine 3-ply – two rough strips of the black stuff, with grass and reeds up the middle! |
| **High Point:** | Corsenside Common 366m. |
| **Maps:** | Ordnance Survey Landranger 80 Cheviot Hills & Kielder Water, Explorer OL42 Kielder Water. |
| | **Facilities:** Space for four cars at the Low Cleughs Bastle car park. Bellingham has shops, two tearoom/cafes, three pubs and a youth hostel. There is also the excellent Bay Horse Inn at West Woodburn. |

## PLOTTING PLAN

| *START:* | Approach | Map Reference | Depart |
|---|---|---|---|
| Low Cleughs Bastle, Low Leam | – | 80/881862$^{1}/_{2}$ | ESE |
| West Woodburn, A68 | WSW | 892$^{1}/_{2}$868 | NW |
| Corsenside XR | S | 889877$^{1}/_{2}$ | WNW |
| Hareshaw Head, B6320 | SE | 851886$^{1}/_{2}$ | SW |
| Pennine Way, Abbey Rigg | NE | 841880 | S |
| Keepers Cottage, B6320 | NE | 836868 | S |
| Bellingham | NE | 839833 | ESE |
| Old Rede Bridge road | SSW | 860830 | NE |
| Hole farm | S | 866$^{1}/_{2}$846$^{1}/_{2}$ | NE |
| *FINISH:* | | | |
| Low Leam layby | W | 881862$^{1}/_{2}$ | – |

## Route Description

This ride started out as a neat, but tough circuit around a classic piece of Northumbrian high ground. Alas the real title should be 'Defeated by Percy's Moss', the long N-S bridleway you see marked on the OS map as the Pennine Way between Hareshaw House and Blakelaw. It turned out to be too wet for bikes, (too wet for anyone really, as commented upon by a long-suffering Dutchman in his book on the Pennine Way *'One Man And His Bog'*!). The alternative using the super-steep farm road out to the B6320, the sustained high speed descent into Bellingham – pronounced Bellingjam by the locals – and renewed acquaintance with the old rally roads in the vicinity of Rede Bridge provided adequate compensation, in fact providing greater variety and probably improving on the original idea.

Chalky White, a good friend but major critic, will probably say I'm using old rally routes again, but in my defence I would point out I'd never been over Corsenside or around the Rede Bridge roads in DAYLIGHT until I started mountain biking! I had no idea what they actually looked like.

### The loop

Start by departing ESE to West Woodburn from the roadside car park, then take care when turning L onto the A68. There is a 30 mph speed limit through West Woodburn but when drivers see the size of the hill you are about to attempt, they tend to put the boot in early. It is 1.14 km uphill from West Woodburn to Corsenside XR, then when you turn L into the gated road that carries you over the summit of Corsenside Common, 366m, it is another 2.55 km to the top. After 1.50 km swing R with the wall and continue with the broken tarmac, lumpy as it is, over the summit and down to the B6320 at Hareshaw Head. We know the level field road looks tempting, but stick with the 3-ply tarmac.

NOTE: There is a satellite stance of the Otterburn Military Ranges for big guns on Corsenside summit. In the highly unlikely event of finding the Corsenside XR – Hareshaw Head road closed, simply continue NNW on the A68 to Old Town XR, turn L onto B6320 SP 'Bellingham' and rejoin the route at Hareshaw Head. This will add 3.73 km to the route, but rob you of the outstanding panoramic view from the top.

From Hareshaw Head ride WSW down the B6320 for 1.03 km looking for the Pennine Way (PW) signpost at the old mine workings. Turn L and follow what is initially good field road up and around the flank of Abbey Rigg for 1.34 km with the PW to Hareshaw House farm. The large old gates near the farm may well be tied, but steps over the wall are provided. On reaching Hareshaw House turn R, downhill, across the Hareshaw Burn and steeply up very broken tarmac to B6320 at Keepers Cottage reached after a further 1.21 km.

Now follow B6320 for 4.03 km down into the centre of Bellingham, the fastest section of the ride. In Bellingham turn L, SP 'Redesmouth', across the bridge then R, SP 'Redesmouth' again, into Russell Terrace and ride parallel to the old railway for 2.48 km to a narrow railway arch, looking to turn L into a wide stony road about 30 metres beyond the bridge.

This old county highway signposted 'Border County Ride', has several gates, but follow the obvious green road roughly NE for 0.92 km to a red gate by a substantial hurdle at a tiny stream bridge where you fork 45 L onto a lesser green track to continue NE to Hole farm. There are tiny signs saying 'Border County Ride' but you probably won't see them until you stop. After an initial steep start this very green road levels out as it heads for Shawbush – not named on the Landranger – 1.19 km away. Turn L along the wall at this lonely old house/shed looking to fork R after 210 metres down to a stony old ford then N to Hole farm. The original stone paving can still be seen in the ancient ford, but it's all a bit green and probably best to dismount. The very deep grass on the opposite side may well reduce you to walking in any case. Follow the field edge past the muck heap then out onto the Bellingham - West Woodburn road where yet another 'Border County Ride' SP points you R back towards the car park. Undulating, but mainly mainly downhill tarmac carries you the final 3.04 km to  Low Cleughs Bastle.

***Percy's Moss.*** *Late afternoon Corsenside Common. Get out of there, you are going to get very wet! An unexpected front came in from the W. Despite unbounded optimism, precipitation was immense. The electricity board recorded 1000 lightening strikes!*

**Roads Round Rubbingstob Hill.** *The water company's road around the S side of Colt Crag reservoir doubles as a bridleway. The approaches to it and later departure are agricultural in extreme, but this is lovely.*

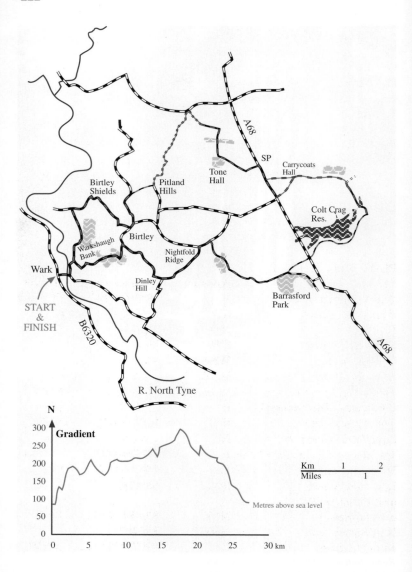

Birtley Shields

Pitland Hills

Tone Hall

SP

Carrycoats Hall

Colt Crag Res.

Birtley

Warkshaugh Bank

Nightfold Ridge

Wark

Dinley Hill

Barrasford Park

START & FINISH

B6320

A68

A68

R. North Tyne

**N**

**Gradient**

300
250
200
150
100
50
0

Metres above sea level

Km 1 2
Miles 1

0 5 10 15 20 25 30 km

## 37    Roads Round Rubbingston Hill

| | | |
|---|---|---|
| **Grade** | 19 Strenuous | |
| **27.06 km** | **(16.82 miles)** | |
| **4.38 km** | Moorland track/path | |
| **1.14 km** | Estate road (Water company) | |
| **21.54 km** | Tarmac – not all visible! | |
| **High Point:** | gate above Lowshieldgreen Crags (Tone Lane) 292m. | |
| **Maps:** | O S Landrangers 87 Hexham & Haltwhistle, 80 Cheviot Hills & Kielder Forest, Explorers OL43 Hadrian's Wall, OL42 Kielder Water. | |
| **Facilities:** | There are three pubs in Wark but the best option – particularly on a nice day – is the Tone Inn, on the A68 where the route crosses for the second time. | |

## PLOTTING PLAN

| *START:* | Approach | Map Reference | Depart |
|---|---|---|---|
| War Memorial Wark | – | 87/860$\frac{1}{2}$770$\frac{1}{2}$ | E |
| Warkshaugh Bank | SW | 869773 | E |
| Dinley Hill | NW | 884774$\frac{1}{2}$ | SE |
| Near Nightfold Ridge | SW | 898775 | NNE |
| Gunnerton Burn | WNW | 912769$\frac{1}{2}$ | E |
| A68 – bridleway crossing | WSW | 928$\frac{1}{2}$774$\frac{1}{2}$ | NE |
| Thockrington road end | WSW | 944$\frac{1}{2}$786$\frac{1}{2}$ | NNW |
| Carrycoats Hall 'triangle' | E | 925797 | SW |
| A68, Check Gate | ENE | 919$\frac{1}{2}$791$\frac{1}{2}$ | NNW |
| Low Farm, Tone Lane | NE | 911799 | NW |
| Tone Hall Cottage, Tone Lane | E | 80/904803 | N |
| Tone Lane end | SE | 896$\frac{1}{2}$815$\frac{1}{2}$ | SW |
| Lowshield Green | NNE | 889800 | SSW |
| near Pitland Hills – | | | |
| onto bridleway | NNE | 87/886794$\frac{1}{2}$ | WSW |
| N of Birtley | NNW | 880787 | S |
| Birtley Shields | E | 870791$\frac{1}{2}$ | WNW |

| | Approach | Map Reference | Depart |
|---|---|---|---|
| above Gold Island | NE | 864$^1$/$_2$777 | S |
| FINISH: Wark | E | 860$^1$/$_2$770$^1$/$_2$ | – |

## Route Description

An intricate network of lanes exists to the E of Wark – sometimes referred to as Wark on Tyne, as opposed to Wark on Tweed in the N of the county – and most of this ride is tarmac based, although quite a lot is 'mountain bike tarmac', in other words it can be very narrow, potholed or covered in mud, and occasionally all three.

Much of the route lies above the 200m contour, but Wark sits at 80m on the River North Tyne. Inevitably the first part of the route climbs stiffly, very stiffly in places, but rest assured you get all of it back in a most sporting fashion!

Depart E out of Wark, across the single-lane bridge over the North Tyne, then TJTL, SP 'Birtley', R away from the river at No Through Road, uphill R again near the top of the first part of the hill, following Birtley once more, over the old railway and eventually slightly down to the black and white chevrons. That was Warkshaugh Bank. Swing L with the main road then stiffly uphill again to the village nameplate at the S end of Birtley. As far as I know this second bank doesn't have a name, but it's just as nasty!

After this everything is easy. Possibly not, but you will probably have time to enjoy the countryside. Turn sharp R just before the village sign and ride SE past Dinley Hill. Turn L after 1.53 km where the road climbs mainly NE towards Gunnerton – but that arm is missing off the fingerpost, best to follow 'Colwell' – up to the junction near Nightfold Ridge. Here you swing R towards 'Colwell' again, then after only 240 metres turn R into skinny single-lane road SP 'Barrasford Park'. This runs SE past Gunnerton Farm for 2.09 km to the junction at Pity Me where you swing L, SP 'Barrasford Park' again and up past the caravan site.

The first stretch of roughstuff starts opposite the main gate of the caravan site, a little-used bridleway emanating from a five-bar gate signposted 'Public Bridleway, A68'. The mud and ruts at the gate soon disappear as you drift gently away from the road at about 30°, then once you reach the brow of the hill you can see the A68 and the rush-fringed line of the bridleway leading to a gated gap in the far wall. You should also be able to see the wooden signpost at the main road.

Care crossing the A68, aim slightly L towards the end of the wall at the reservoir. The blue bridleway arrow gives a good indication of the ride angle. After 0.57 km (0.35 mile) you reach the gate onto the good gravel reservoir road. Follow the S side of Colt Crag Reservoir all the way around to the gate at the N end of the dam, then aim to continue NE, to the R of the trees, then R with the field road past the drinking troughs and across to the tarmac road you should see coming down from Thockrington.

On joining tarmac again turn L, SP 'Carrycoats', over the brow to more gates – take the R option between substantial stone walls, rather lumpy – across the eastern extremity of the reservoir, up the skinny undulating three-ply to the 'moorland' junction after 1.27 km (0.79 mile). Turn L, SP 'Birtley, Wark' and head W to the Carrycoats 'triangle'. Looking at the map you might wonder why we don't ride straight on to the A68, instead of swinging SW as now shown. In fact the SO option is the more interesting road, but unfortunately the junction with the A68 occurs about 50 metres from a blind brow – which you will see when you ride NNW to the Tone Inn. So we swing SW to the A68 at Check Gate, then turn R, over the offending brow, then L between the buildings of the Tone Inn complex, signposted 'Public Right of Way'.

Follow the tree-lined Tone Lane roughly NW for 1.22 km to Tone Hall Cottage, turn R before the gates onto a rougher road which heads due N, then roughly NW to a gate above Lowshieldgreen Crags, the highest point on the route, 292m. Here the lane celebrates by becoming a grassy green track which flashes down to the walled junction with the Bellingham road.

Don't go through the gate at the bottom, turn sharp L onto some of the best single-track tarmac in Northumberland, down through Lowshield Green and on towards Pitland Hills. Look to turn R onto the wide bridleway after 2.45 km about 150 metres N of the farm. There are two fingerposts at the gate, one for a footpath the other for our bridleway. Keep R and follow the muddy/stony track next to the wall on the R. The wide track doesn't last long. Keep to the higher ground above the valley, then follow the best sheep track down to the stream by the gate after 0.76 km.

TJTL when you reach the tarmac, then follow the single-lane road roughly S to Birtley. The uphill gradient might come as a bit of a shock. The obvious thing to do when you reach the outskirts of Birtley might be to shoot straight down to the river, but for the final excursion turn R, SP 'Birtley', then R again after 100 metres SP 'Birtley Shields'. This is Piper Lane. Turn sharp R after a further 400 metres, actually following the public road when the farm road is wider, eventually riding around to the widest gate in the county at Birtley Shields. There are several more gates on this road so always ensure you can stop within the distance you can see to be clear, as two or three are hidden around corners. Much of the descent is broken and loose. Look out for the junction on the L after 1.88 km. We turn L up past Thorneyhirst and it is easy to overshoot and find yourself hurtling down to Low Carry House. (OK, I got carried away and missed it!) The final wiggle takes you down through the old railway, along an elevated section above Gold Island, on to a Give Way where you turn R, SP 'Wark', down to the river and back along the outbound route into Wark. Total distance 27.06 km. It may well have felt like more! Downhill tarmac carries you the final 3.04 km to Low Cleughs

***Right: Castles, Climbs & Clarts.*** *Haresby Road, between Whinnetley Moss and Thorngrafton. This clarty track may look like a Roman road and probably is. A cache of Roman gold coins was found near the 13th tree on the L ... so it it said!*

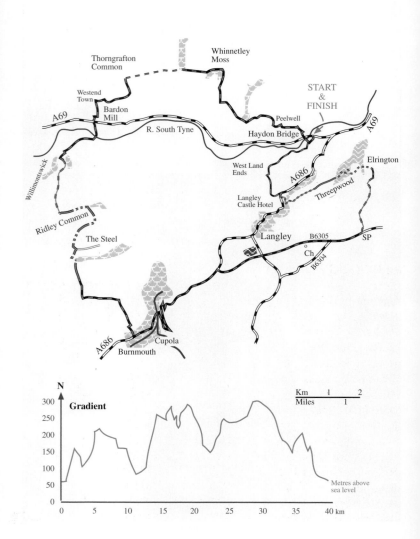

# 38    Castles, Climbs & Clarts

| | |
|---|---|
| **Grade** | 21 A real test! Expert category. |
| **39.64 km** | **(24.63 miles)** |
| **11.38 km** | Unsealed county roads. |
| **28.26 km** | Tarmac, including a high percentage of single lane, some of it three-ply. |
| **High Point:** | north of the river – Haresby Road, 212m, south of the river – near Stublick Chimney, 299m. |
| **Maps:** | Ordnance Survey Landranger 87 Hexham & Haltwhistle, Explorer OL43 Hadrian's Wall. |
| **Facilities:** | Haydon Bridge has three pubs, fish and chip shop, shops and caravan/campsite, Cart's Bog Inn, Langley Castle, everything from coffee all day to B&B. Railway stations at Haydon Bridge and Bardon Mill (Newcastle – Carlisle line.) |

## PLOTTING PLAN

| *START:* | Approach | Map Reference | Depart |
|---|---|---|---|
| Haydon Bridge F C car park | – | 87/845645 | S |
| Bridge over River South Tyne | SE | 843642$^1$/$_2$ | NW |
| Peelwell | S | 833648 | N |
| Honeycrook Burn | SE | 822$^1$/$_2$650 | NW |
| Haresby Road, | | | |
| Whinnetley Moss | ENE | 814663 | W |
| Thorngrafton | E | 783654 | W |
| Bardon Mill, then | | | |
| footbridge over S. Tyne | N | 781646 | S |
| Willimontswick | NE | 771636$^1$/$_2$ | SE |
| Ridley Common (N) | NNW | 771610$^1$/$_2$ | NE |
| Ridley Common (S) 279m | NE | 777615$^1$/$_2$ | SW |
| Rowside | W | 781596 | E |
| A686, Burnmouth | NNW | 793584$^1$/$_2$ | NE |
| A686/B6305 Cart's Bog | SW | 817604$^1$/$_2$ | E |

|                              | Approach | Map Reference | Depart |
|------------------------------|----------|---------------|--------|
| Stublick Chimney, B6305      | SW       | 840612        | ENE    |
| B6305 near Blackhall Pike    | WSW      | 859615        | N      |
| Elrington                    | S        | 862634        | W      |
| Threepwood                   | ENE      | 851631        | WSW    |
| Castle Farm                  | ENE      | 833626½       | N      |
| East Land Ends               | W        | 839639        | E      |
| *FINISH:*                    |          |               |        |
| Haydon Bridge car park       | S        | 845645        | –      |

Castles, in the shape of Willimontswick and Langley – much restored – form part of the historic side of the ride, plus of course Staward Peel, which you will see on the map to the N of what in motoring terms was one of the most tortuous and spectacular climbs in the county, Cupola Bank, but compared with the terrain we cover simply a sustained slog. 'Staward-le-Peel' is listed in Murray's 'Handbook for Travellers in Durham and Northumberland' of 1890 as 'a famous resort for picnics', but very little now remains of the peel tower and Staward railway station – presumably the stop on the Hexham-Allendale railway used by the Victorians – has been a private house for many years. Older historic links can be made en-route to Thorngrafton, where, in 1837, a small bronze vessel was found containing 63 Roman coins, the latest being from the time of Hadrian, so keep your eyes peeled! Even older – probably – is the stone circle at The Steel on Ridley Common. It is the biggest in Northumberland, but two of the stones look relatively new, perhaps Victorian replacements. Strangely, it doesn't appear on the OS maps. For those interested in industrial archaeology, Stublick Chimney, highest point on the entire route, is the place. Try standing in the doorway and feel the draw even on a still day.

Climbs are numerous! The first group rise from river level at Haydon Bridge to Whinnetley Moss in a series of steps to 209m, the hardest in the village itself! Payback comes from Thorngrafton Common down to Bardon Mill. Next comes the gated road from Willimontswick to the N side of Ridley Common, most of which is three-ply, one section being also grassy and stony. You will see two sets of double arrows on the map as you pass the stone circle at The Steel, but they aren't the full story. This entire road is either steep down or steeply up, a total switchback rising and dipping across the 250m contour no less than five times! In addition to Cupola Bank the flog up to Stublick Chimney can grind on a bit, but is often eased by a following westerly wind. Then, apart from a sharp 'click' in the woods near Threepwood, it is all downhill after the chimney.

Clarts are not confined to the old county roads, but here they are guaranteed. Haresby Road, from Whinnetley Moss to Thorngrafton Common has ford marked on the Explorer at about two thirds distance, but it turned out to be minor compared to some of the previous pools. The Willimontswick grassy section can be very slimy, but the long hill from Lonninghead Plantation down to the A686 at Burnmouth has a bit of everything. November probably wasn't the best time to ride it if keeping the bike clean had been a priority, but thereafter there was no disguising the quality of the route. Except for the gate off the B6305 all the others down to Elrington were open, which made this high speed speckled run the highlight, but the sweeping bends in the woods between Elrington and Threepwood came a close second. Clartiest bit of the whole route can be a single field between Threepwood and Langley Castle, but all is forgiven in the steep downhill back to the A686. Leafy, rutted, stony, slippery, it is all there. Final bit of roughstuff runs downhill again, from Castle Farm, Langley to West Land Ends. It is dead straight but takes considerable courage to let it rip.

**Route Instructions**

Start by riding S from the riverside football field car park, back to A69, straight across – when safe – into the S side of the village, along to the Anchor Inn, then turn R across the old bridge after 280 metres. You could simply turn R onto A69 then R again at the Railway Hotel, but you might find yourself standing in the middle of the main Newcastle-

Carlisle trunk road waiting for a gap. The bridge loop forces you to walk down to the A69 after crossing the bridge and wait for a good gap, and also lets you check the opening times of the fish & chip shop.

Ride N to the railway crossing at Haydon Bridge station then straight on up North Bank, past the school to the Peelwell junction on a bend after 1.21 km. Turn L, SP 'Chesterwood', then swing R at Haydon View, up to another TJ with a grey seat after 0.55 km where you turn L then L again after only 90 metres into a narrower road which actually goes downhill. After 0.89 km keep R at the deceptive triangle at Hill House, down and straight on over the little bridge with 'No Track Laying Vehicles', then up again to the Whinnetley junction after 0.98 km. Turn R uphill yet again SP 'Public Byway, Haresby Road' to top out at Whinnetley Moss after 1.08 km. We're not sure whether it is a good idea or not, but if you turn around and look slightly E of due S you will see Stublick Chimney on the distant skyline. You are standing within a few metres of the highest point on the N side of the river, the chimney is the highest point on the route on the S. We only hope your reaction is good, if not you can cut and run at Bardon Mill!

Turn L onto Haresby Road, red byway arrows and No Through Road sign, and ride W for 3.11 km on mainly good three-ply dirt to the junction on Thorngrafton Common. Turn L down narrow tarmac at the far end, R at the first bend, through Thorngrafton, then L downhill again with the main road at Westend Town. At the TJ after 2.32 km turn L, SP 'Bardon Mill, under the A69, down to the old A69 in Bardon Mill. Then straight on as you can SP 'Ash Farm' on a narrow lane that leads to the railway crossing. Obey the British Rail instructions for crossing the line, then around to the long footbridge on a rough track. Attempting to follow the line of the old road through the river is not recommended. At the far end of the footbridge turn R with the narrow tarmac road and follow to the castellated farm at Willimontswick, reached after 2.01 km. Turn L over the crest before the farm, as directed by red byway arrows, then after an initial dip to a gate it is uphill for 1.32 km on tarmac, then stony road, then grass to the Allensgreen road end.

Straight ahead, uphill again for a further 0.60 km on 3-ply tarmac to the TJ on the N side of Ridley Common, where you turn L and across the cattle grid on Winshield Side, then after 0.92 km look for a junction on the R, SP 'Whitfield', and a hand painted 'East & West Steel'. This is the super-switchback road that will carry you past Shankhead, the stone circle at The Steel – watch the angled cattle grid at the Kingswood Burn – and on past Huntershield to the TJ after 3.40 km where you turn L past another irresistible No Through Road sign. Narrow tarmac carries you downhill for 1.09 km to the rough road down the side of Lonninghead Plantation, on the R immediately before the gate to Dodd Bank farm. In addition to the natural hazards of the lane, some of the biggest pheasants in the land are very prone to zooming across your path!

Burnmouth, on A686, heralds a spell of civilisation as you turn hairpin L towards Cupola Bank. Follow this road roughly NE for 4.94 km to the Cart's Bog junction where you turn R onto B6305, signposted 'Hexham', ENE through the offset crossroads at Langley Dam after 1.43 km, then on past Stublick Chimney after a further 1.14 km of sustained, but gentler climbing, then L, SP 'Hexham' again, still with B6305, when the B6304 joins from the R, for a further 1.00 km before turning off L onto the old county road SP 'Byway, Elrington'.

Close the green gate after you, and hope that you are as lucky as the day of the official ride and find all the others open, but don't bank on it! 2.06 km of downhill stony road takes you to Elrington railway bridge, then look to turn L through the farm, SP 'Byway, Threepwood' for more of the same. Keep R, downhill past the farm and look for the next junction near Dinnetley just after the refurbished waterfall bridge at 0.82 km. The options are, L to R, a track up to the farm, a five-bar gate into a field, and a five-bar gate into the woods. Take the last, then swing R down through the trees, weaving L and R down over an old stone bridge, up a surprisingly steep little hill, then skirt Threepwood on a good stony road. Straight on past this large farm after 0.82 km again, heading mainly SW for Langley Castle on A686. When the avenue of trees ends, follow the field road through the gates, swap sides of the wall for the squelchy bit, then back again onto good grass and finally down through the trees to A686 opposite the castle.

Turn R onto A686 for only 100 metres, then L, SP 'West Deanraw' and slightly uphill to Castle Farm after 0.52 km where you swing R then go straight ahead at the next corner, SP 'Public Byway, West Land Ends'. This is the final stretch of roughstuff, fittingly downhill, loose and rutted, but make sure you can turn TJTR at the bottom, then R again at the bottom of the next little tarmac hill and finally NE along past East Land Ends into Haydon Bridge (South). Cross A69 with care after 2.59 km and back to the car park. Total distance 39.64 km.

***Right: Makemerich & Frolic.*** *Ferny Chesters farm and Shaftoe Crags from the route near A696 at Edgehouse. Rain imminent.*

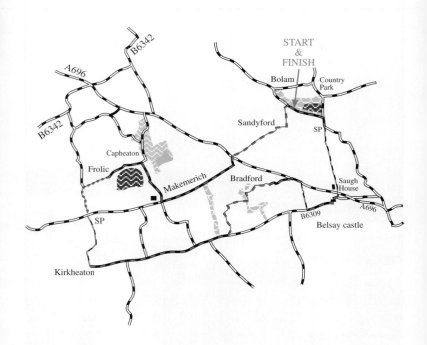

B6342
A696
B6342
START
&
FINISH
Bolam
Country
Park
Sandyford
SP
Capheaton
Frolic
Makemerich
Bradford
Saugh
House
B6309
A696
SP
Belsay castle
Kirkheaton

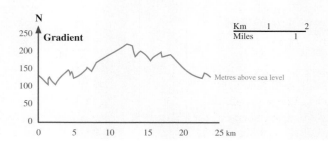

**N**

**Gradient**

Metres above sea level

Km    1        2
Miles      1

250
200
150
100
50
0

0    5    10    15    20    25 km

# 39    Makemerich & Frolic

| | |
|---|---|
| **Grade** | 14 Energetic |
| **23.59 km** | **(14.65 miles)** |
| **3.49 km** | Field path |
| **3.85 km** | Farm track |
| **0.16 km** | Farm road |
| **16.09 km** | Tarmac |
| **High point:** | Kirkheaton 219m. |
| **Maps:** | Ordnance Survey Landrangers 81 Alnwick & Morpeth, 87 Hexham & Haltwhistle, 88 Newcastle upon Tyne. Explorer OL 42 Kielder Water, 316 Newcastle upon Tyne, 325 Morpeth & Blyth. |
| **Facilities:** | Space for 10 cars at West Wood car park, Bolam Lake, (START) £1.00 all day. Tea and light refreshments served at Capheaton village hall weekends and Bank Holidays throughout the summer – although this is a voluntary scheme and may be discontinued at any time. Best carry your own bait. |

## PLOTTING PLAN

| *START:* | Approach | Map Reference | Depart |
|---|---|---|---|
| West Wood car park | | | |
| Bolam Lake | – | 81/076818 | ESE |
| How Burn bridge | N | 084$^1$/$_2$810 | S |
| River Blyth footbridge | | | |
| (& onto OS 88) | NNW | 086$^1$/$_2$801$^1$/$_2$ | S |
| Saugh House farm | N | 88/087796 | S |
| B6309 – bridleway – A696 | ENE | 079790 | N |
| Bradford road (& onto OS 87) | E | 072798 | WSW |
| Bradford Lodge (pond) | NE | 87/064795 | SW |
| Belsay road, spot height 174m | ENE | 056$^1$/$_2$783 | WSW |
| Kirkheaton – onto bridleway | ENE | 020775 | NNW |

| | Approach | Map Reference | Depart |
|---|---|---|---|
| River Blyth (again) | | | |
| wooden bridge | S | 021783 | NNW |
| Frolic (& onto OS 81) | SW | 025799$^{1}/_{2}$ | NE |
| Capheaton | | | |
| (& back onto OS 87) | WSW | 81/034$^{1}/_{2}$803 | SSE |
| Makemerich XR | | | |
| (& onto OS 81) | NNW | 87/040792$^{1}/_{2}$ | ENE |
| A696 near Edgehouse | S | 81/059805 | NE |
| Sandyford 'triangle' | WSW | 073$^{1}/_{2}$813 | N |
| FINISH: | | | |
| West Wood car park | NW | 076818 | – |

## Route Description

The Blyth was one of the great coal rivers of Northumberland, exporting hundreds of thousands of tons over the years. There was also a thriving shipyard and at one time an important submarine base. Today the bauxite handling plant and timber imports are the mainstays of commercial shipping, and sited just off the mouth of the river are the first sea-sited wind turbines in the county.

A mere 25 km inland the River Blyth has a totally different look. Here, weaving its way through our bike route, is a small fairly insignificant country stream, too small even for the fishers of brown trout, dammed to make a farm pond, used by cattle as a source of water, but still requiring substantial bridges to allow the farmers access to the fields and within 1500 metres of its source having one of the first land-based wind turbines in Northumberland.

This route didn't set out to be a tour of the nascent River Blyth, more a run around some of the least frequented roads in the county, but en route provides one of the greatest variations of surface in the book. There is ample opportunity to clean out the tyres on the tarmac ready for the next bit of off-road, but rides a couple of grades harder than it appears on the map!

There are three car parks at Bolam Lake. If West Wood is full use one of the others, it will only add two or three hundred metres to the ride. We start at West Wood car park because it is directly on the route. Depart SE along the side of the lake, swing R with the main road at Bolam Low House, then downhill, looking to go straight on – with care – at the next bend, into a field road SP 'Bridleway, Saugh House', 0.93 km gone and you're into it. You now head S for 2.09 km to A696 at Saugh House farm. Good twin-track takes you to a surprise tarmac road crossing, where it is straight on up a grassy field to a gate on the crest of the hill. Aim for the farm keeping the fence on your L, then straight on again at the next road through two gates bearing Right of Way plates. The going becomes rougher, then over the footbridge and up to Saugh House, taking care through the farmyard and crossing the A696.

The gate at the far side of the main road has a tricky catch – use both hands – then turn R onto the B6309 at the far side of the field, through the bends and look to turn R again after 1.03 km into a field road bridleway that sometimes has a muck heap at the start. A fingerpost 'Bridleway, Jedburgh Road' confirms the route very grassy over the first brow, a wet sump at the old metal gate which seems permanently open, then grassy again down to the A696. After 0.81 km turn L along the main road for only 240 metres to the tarmac Bradford farm road – SP missing at the time of writing. Then straight on through the farm looking to fork L after 1.27 km, at Bradford Lodge, along the S side of the pond to a cattle grid at South Bradford. Keep R and head SW through a galvanised gate towards the wood on a dirt road, where you turn L along the edge. Then R through the shelter belt just after a crest and along to a gate reached after 1.22 km.

Once through the gate the road becomes grassier, the stream bounding the road on the R is the River Blyth. Swing R to the first line of trees, L uphill before the green gate, over the crest and S to the Belsay road after 0.89 km. Turn R onto the tarmac and ride W for 4.25 km to Kirkheaton, at the end of the No Through Road.

A bridleway fingerpost devoid of destination points the way across the field beyond a pair of huge metal gates at Kirkheaton. You can see the little white 'bridleway' plate on the far gate, which takes you through to another gate, then another, then after 400 metres look for a white 'bridleway' disc on a wicket gate in the fence on the R. There is no track as such, but in a certain light you may be able to discern a mark across to the fence. Ride out from under the sycamore at 45° aiming to join the fence at the angle. Then ride on to the gate in the corner – bridleway plate – turn L through the gate and head N to cross an even smaller River Blyth at a large wooden bridge. Bumpy on the approach. Keep heading N over the ridge eventually reaching the XR leading to White House after 1.26 km – it seems further!

It is now tarmac – of highly differing qualities – all the way to the finish.

Straight on over the cattle grid, SP 'Kirkharle', then after 0.84 km of 3-ply turn R into a wide walled entrance, through the green gate, and downhill on even lesser, unfenced three-ply to the wood. You are greeted by a wooden five-bar gate sporting one of the biggest and finest latches in the land, harnessed to a pair of fine stone stoups (gateposts). This is a rare example of the estate blacksmith's art. Broken three-ply flanked by trees carries you up past Frolic, on past St. Edward's Lake, where autumnal geese fresh from the Arctic honked my puny efforts on the bike and on to Capheaton after 1.87 km. An archetypal tree set in a grass triangle marks the junction where you turn R, signposted 'Stamfordham'. Then 1.32 km to the S you reach Makemerich XR where the only SP for us turning L is the 3T weight limit. However, we get the best road, flanked by mature beech trees, with two so close to the single track road one may speculate upon the chances of a coach and four-in-hand getting through at anything more than a brisk walk! After 2.48 km you reach the A696 again.

Care crossing the main road, follow the tarred field road NE for 1.79 km past Sandyford to the little grass 'triangle', then N over a well spaced cattle grid to the final TJ another 0.72 km farther on. Turn R and 420 metres later you reach West Wood car park.

***Featherstone, South Tyne.*** *Trail between Featherstone Park Stn & Coanwood. Believe it or not, this grand piece of railway architecture does no more than connect pastures on opposite sides of the line!*

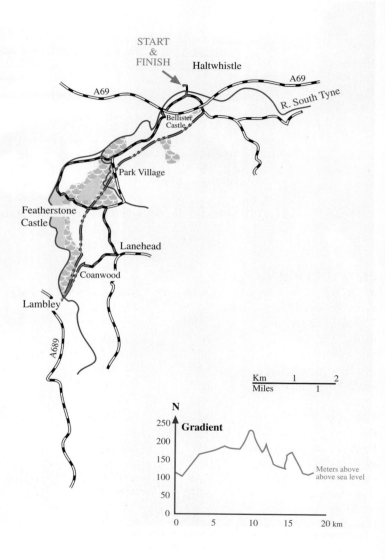

START & FINISH

Haltwhistle

A69

A69

R. South Tyne

Bellister Castle

Park Village

Featherstone Castle

Lanehead

Coanwood

Lambley

A689

Km | 1 | 2
Miles | 1

N

Gradient

250
200
150
100
50
0

Meters above above sea level

0    5    10    15    20 km

## 40    Featherstone, South Tyne

| | |
|---|---|
| **Grade** | 10 Sporting |
| **18.02 km** | **(11.20 miles)** |
| **7.54 km** | Rail trail |
| **10.48 km** | Rural tarmac. |
| **High Point:** | Lanehead, Coanwood 232m. |
| **Maps:** | Ordnance Survey Landranger 86 Haltwhistle, or 87 Hexham & Haltwhistle (big overlap), Explorer OL43 Hadrian's Wall. |
| **Facilities:** | Free parking at Haltwhistle railway station and just off Main Street in Haltwhistle itself. Being the 'Centre of Britain' there are small hotels, B&Bs, cafés, restaurants and one of the best and most helpful Tourist Information Centres in the land – tel. 01434 322 002 |

## PLOTTING PLAN

| *START:* | Approach | Map reference | Depart |
|---|---|---|---|
| Haltwhistle railway station | – | 86/704638 | NE then S |
| Plenmeller Road onto | | | |
| South Tyne Trail | N | 709$^1$/$_2$632 | SW |
| South Tyne Trail/'dismtd rly' | NE | 691620 | SW |
| Featherstone Station | NE | 681$^1$/$_2$607 | SSW |
| Lambley Viaduct | NNE | 675584 | NNE |
| Coanwood | SW | 680592$^1$/$_2$ | E |
| Lanehead | W | 688595$^1$/$_2$ | NNW |
| Rowfoot | S | 685607 | W |
| Featherstone Bridge End | SW | 675618$^1$/$_2$ | ENE |
| Bellister Castle | | | |
| ( L & R under A69) | SSW | 699$^1$/$_2$631$^1$/$_2$ | NW |
| Bellister Road | SW | 703635 | NE |
| *FINISH:* | | | |
| Haltwhistle railway station | N | 703638 | – |

## Route Description

South Tyne might sound like Newcastle area, but nothing could be more different. The confluence of the Rivers North and South Tyne lies some 41.7 km upstream to the W of 'The Toon', then add a further 26.5 km and you reach Haltwhistle, our start point. The ride heads a little further W then S with the River South Tyne to the northern extremity of the Pennines, while the river itself continues farther S actually being born on the slopes of Cross Fell in Cumbria, the highest point in the Pennine Chain. From this you might well expect the terrain to be hilly, and it is, fiercely hilly. All the other rides to this SW district start with a tough hill, a fact of life, but this loop goes some way to redressing the balance. It does actually rise 80m between Haltwhistle and the Coanwood car park but takes 6.55 km of very gentle railway gradient to do it. Destination of the ride is the restored Lambley Viaduct, a magnificent railway structure 263.8m long and 32.6m high from the river to trackbed at the highest point. You ride as far as the viaduct then retrace for 680 metres to start the tarmac return journey via the ride high point of 232m at Lanehead, Coanwood, down past Featherstone Castle, Bellister Castle and for much of the way alongside the River South Tyne which once more enjoys a reputation as a fine salmon river.

## Haltwhistle railway station to Lambley Viaduct.

The 'depart' directions of 'N, E then S' on the Plotting Plan might look crazy, but you ride out of the old railway station yard, turn immediately R (E) then R (S) again SP 'Pennine Cycleway, Alston', under the railway bridge, across the River South Tyne, L at Bellister Road and around to the new bypass. Until the 1960s this was the main road out of town to the south.

Care when crossing the realigned A69, now an offset XR for us, turn R then immediately L, SP 'Whitfield', looking to turn R onto the obvious old railway atop the embankment through a bridle gate with very discreet signs for the South Tyne Trail. A narrow rising path gets you up onto the old trackbed, then it's a straightforward ride all the way to Lambley Viaduct. You ride under bridges that do no more than give access to pastures, past ditches of water pure enough to support cress, then care after 3.25 km when crossing the main road at Park Village – follow 'NCR 68' and down onto the railway again. Care again after a further 1.11 km at Featherstone Park station, especially in view of the fact you will be coming down the hill later in the ride, but on this first occasion follow SP 'Alston 12'. The final road crossing of the outbound leg comes 1.34 km later, at Coanwood car park, this time follow the wooden SP 'Lambley Viaduct, South Tyne Trail', NOT 'Pennine Cycleway'. This starts as narrow tree-lined single track but soon widens, particularly when you ride through Coanwood Station car park where there are gates and another fingerpost SP 'Lambley Viaduct'. Leave your bikes at the end and walk out onto the structure – there is no through route.

### Lambley Viaduct to Featherstone and Haltwhistle

Retrace to Coanwood Station car park, but fork R this time into a narrow stony lane that carries you up to Coanwood. Swing R, still uphill SP 'Lanehead' on the 'main' road past the little school which had – or probably still has – a beautiful old notice extolling the virtues of the 'Three Rs – Reading, Writing and Rithmatic'. After 2.00 km you reach Lanehead where the main road swings L down to Featherstone Rowfoot some 1.35 km (0.84 mile) distant. Here TL, SP 'Featherstone Park', a narrow single-track road down past the Wallace Arms – temptations abound – across the outbound route, up a sharp rise, then steeply down past Featherstone Castle which dates back to the original tower built by Thomas de Featherstonehaugh in the 1320s.

Local legend has it that Abigail Featherstonehaugh, a daughter of the family, sometime in the late 1600s was due to marry the son of a local Baron, but classically was in love with one of the neighbouring Ridleys. However, on the night of the wedding, as the wedding party rode the bounds of the estate, which was apparently the custom, young Ridley launched an attack, the bridegroom put up a good fight but all were killed in the fray. Later that night – at midnight to be exact – the sound of hooves were heard outside the castle, the door of the banqueting hall burst open and the ghostly apparition of Abigail and the rest of the party entered. It is said that even the Baron fainted. It is claimed that the ghostly wedding party can still be seen each 17th January in Pynkin's Cleugh – on the N side of Featherstone Bridge – so either complete the ride before dark or stick to the S side of the river!

Ride straight on past the tall Featherstone Bridge for 1.30 km, up the final steep hill, past the caravan site, joining the main road at the top where you turn L, SP 'Haltwhistle'. Then after another 200 metres of gentle climbing it is down, down all the way to Bellister Castle, which you see perched on a knoll off to the R just before the A69. Virtually opposite the castle entrance TL over a cattle grid, then immediately keep L again to a wooden gate leading onto a concrete road. There is a SP 'Public Bridleway, Haltwhistle' but you probably won't see it until you stop at the gate! This purpose built thoroughfare carries you under the A69 to rejoin the original Bellister Road, now a huge wide strip of empty tarmac. If you pause under the A69 bridge you may well see a dipper, one of our more elusive water birds. He/she always seems to be there, an excellent reflection of the quality of the water in the South Tyne. Finally ride back along to the Blue Bridge, where you first crossed the South Tyne and back into Haltwhistle.

# The Ernest Press Mountain Bike Guide series

Inverness, the Great
Glen & Cairngorms:
**£8.50**

**SCOTLAND,
VOLUME 1
COMING SOON!**

North Wales: **£8.25**

Mid-Wales & the
Marshes: **£7.50**

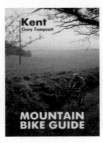

Kent: **£6.95**

Wiltshire: **£8.50**

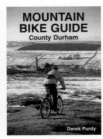

County Durham:
**£7.50**

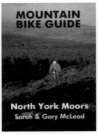

North York Moors:
**£7.50**

Peak District &
Derbyshire: **£8.50**

## Browse and buy online at www.ernest-press.co.uk

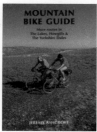

The Lake District, Howgills & York-shire Dales: **£9.00**

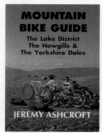

More routes in the Lakes, Howgills & ...
**£8.50**

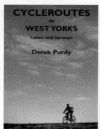

Cycleroutes in West Yorks – Lanes and by-ways: **£7.50**

West Yorkshire:
**£7.00**

Mid Yorkshire, Rye Dale & the Wolds:
**£7.50**

West Midlands:
**£8.00**

East Midlands:
**£7.95**

North Midlands:
**£8.50**

The Peak District & Derbyshire: **£7.50**